Show Jumping

Officers' Hobby into International Sport

Eddie Macken and Pele runners-up in the 1974
World Championship at Hickstead

Show Jumping

Officers' Hobby into
International Sport

Pamela
Macgregor-Morris

David & Charles
Newton Abbot · London
Vancouver

St Martin's Press
New York

ISBN 0 7153 6763 3

Library of Congress Catalog Card Number 75-15378

First published in Great Britain in 1975
and in the United States in 1976.

Printed in Great Britain
for David & Charles (Holdings) Limited
Brunel House, Newton Abbot, Devon

Published in the United States of America
by St Martin's Press, Inc.,
175 Fifth Avenue, New York, NY 10010

Published in Canada
by Douglas David & Charles Limited
1875 Welch Street, North Vancouver, BC

Contents

1 In the Beginning 1868~1914

Although show jumping has a universal appeal to the man in the street it is by no means every horseman's *beau ideal*. Some enjoy a love-hate relationship with the sport, others find it agreeable solely at top international level, but only those who have competed find it invariably interesting on the purely national level.

To the late Captain Lionel Dawson, RN, the legendary and most erudite hunting correspondent of the century, it was 'the most debased form of equestrianism'. Few hunting people find show jumping to their taste, probably because they are doers rather than watchers. The majority of country people, moreover, think jumping over red and white poles a fairly contrived and artificial activity. And a well-known major-general, late of one of the top cavalry regiments, neatly dismissed the sport as 'a means of keeping our NCOs amused while we were playing polo'.

Yet, to millions of armchair riders, televised show jumping is a compulsive spectator sport, while to those involved in it, at whatever level, it holds a perpetually stimulating fascination. The late Colonel Fred Ahern, who was in charged of the Irish Army jumping team, viewed it as an aesthetic art form. 'Each round', he used to tell his riders, 'must be memorable for its beauty.'

There can be no doubt that show jumping on the international plane is indeed a classic equestrian activity – less traditional than racing or foxhunting, but classic none the less. Like any other competitive sport, however, it depends for its interest upon expertise. The basic ingredients are the course, the horse and the rider. If the course is dull, unimaginative or insufficiently testing of the standard of training and proficiency, both of horse and rider, then it fails abysmally in its primary function, which is to entertain. If the horses lack ability or are deficient in schooling, and if the riders are inefficient, a jumping competition degenerates into an exercise in timber felling which is tedious for the spectators and punishing for the participants. In contrast, to watch a well-schooled horse who is a natural jumper and clearly loves his job, ridden smoothly and sympathetically, mastering all the problems inherent in a Grand Prix course and putting up a flowing and fluent performance, is an experience that few who appreciate good horsemanship can easily forget.

International show jumping has reached a degree of sophistication that could never have been prophesied by the pioneers of the sport. Show jumping originated in the second half of the nineteenth century, though men and horses had been jumping fences in the hunting field for at least a hundred years.

In 1868, a competition for a 'high leap' and a 'wide leap' was included in the first horse show of the Royal Dublin Society to test the qualification of horses for the hunting field. On the last day of the show there was a championship over a stone wall for a silver cup and a prize of £10, for which horses had to qualify by clearing the high leap at 4ft 10in. The high leap was described as a fence 'similar to that in use at Islington Show', which presupposes that jumping competitions had already been held in London, at the Royal Agricultural Hall in Islington. The fence in question was three bars, on pivots, trimmed with gorse. The wide leap was a pair of parallel hurdles. The championship stone wall was described by a press correspondent at the time as 'a wall five feet ten inches, jumped in cold blood, off wet sawdust, in a crowded court-yard'. The judging rule was simple, stating that 'the obstacle should be cleared to the satisfaction of the judges'.

Capt. Lionel Dawson (right) and Col Fred Ahern who represented the poles of opinion on show jumping

Jumping soon became a popular form of entertainment, and the competitions progressed from one fence to a short course of fences, some six or eight in number. In 1881 a course of permanent fences – a double bank, a water jump and a stone wall – was laid out and in use at the Royal Dublin Society's new show ground at Ball's Bridge. A year later it was extended to comprise a ditch and bank, stone wall, hurdle, double bank and water jump. All the fences were unrelated and there was no question of riding the course as a whole; it was simply a collection of obstacles, each to be treated as a separate entity. In New York, the National Horse Show first took place in 1883, in Madison Square Garden, and three jumping competitions were held in conjunction with the Paris Olympics in 1900, two of which were won by Belgium and the other by France.

By the turn of the century, though still in its infancy, show jumping had become an established sport, chiefly the preserve of cavalry officers. At this time, the principle of jumping fences on a horse derived from the style then prevalent in the hunting field. The rider leant forward on taking off, and then sat back on landing. The man who was to change all this was the Italian instructor Federico Caprilli who, having passed out of the cavalry school at Modena, devoted the rest of his too-short life – he died in a fall when he was thirty-nine – to a study of the mechanics of the horse and the correct position of the rider. His conclusions were a radical departure from the doctrines of the classical school, and from them originated the 'forward seat', a style which was soon to spread all over the world, revolutionising educated riding, particularly over fences. Caprilli was an even greater student of the psychology of the horse than of seat, balance and centres of gravity. 'He seldom failed to find amusement in his weightiest ponderings,' wrote his disciple and translator, Major Piero Santini. 'His most original combination of duty and play was the fitting to the back of his favourite mare – his inseparable companion in the experiments – of a straw-stuffed dummy of the kind used in all armies for sabre or bayonet practice. Left to her own devices in the stable yard at Tor di Quinto, the cavalry school, with this life-sized puppet on her back, the mare entered wholeheartedly into the spirit of a game of tag with the troopers, while her owner studied her movements in her efforts to escape the encircling soldiers, and the manikin's reactions thereto.'

Another great instructor of the last century was the English classicist, James Fillis, who had a profound influence on dressage riding all over the world. In Russia, his amazing feats as a high-school rider with a circus – which included cantering his horse backwards on three legs – made such an impression that he was invited to take the post of *écuyer en chef* at the cavalry school. It was there that Colonel Paul Rodzianko of the Imperial Guard saw the most remarkable performance of high-school work he had ever witnessed. 'The beauty and ease of his horsemanship was incredible,' he wrote. 'So it was that I became a pupil of James Fillis and my life as a horseman began.'

Colonel Rodzianko's name was to run through sixty years of show jumping like a golden thread. 'He has influenced modern show jumping more than any other rider,' Captain Jack Webber, the BSJA chairman, commented recently, 'and will be remembered for all time as a great instructor and an outstanding personality.'

In the 1900s, having trained with Fillis for a year, Rodzianko was attached to the Russian Embassy in Rome. There he went to see the cavalry school at Tor di Quinto which had been reorganised by Caprilli. 'I watched the officers' performances cross-country with amazement. It was almost incredible that horses and riders should be able to negotiate such obstacles. The ease with which they went over the most dangerous jumps made me pause to consider. Fillis's training had helped me understand a great deal of the science of equitation, but his whole interest really lay in light, free and beautiful high-school work. Although his training in no way interfered with a horse's usefulness in the country, he never obtained results such as these in the open. I talked with Captain Caprilli, who had had a severe struggle to work out and enforce his methods in Italy, and had finally gained complete success. Over six feet tall with a strong, lithe physique, Caprilli was one of the finest men imaginable. He told me: "There is no doubt that Fillis is the greatest master of high-school, but I do not agree with his principles for cross-country riding as there is too much artificial balance. I try to develop the natural balance of the horse."'

Rodzianko obtained the tsar's permission to

complete the eighteen-month course at the Italian cavalry school, during which time he had over a hundred falls, was sometimes black and blue all over and hardly able to move after being rolled on. Sometimes they left the school and rode out in the surrounding countryside, where the horses proved to be as agile as mountain goats. At an old *castello* they used to jump through the ruined windows and go straight downhill, the horses slithering down small cliffs and straight 30ft drops. 'There were uncomfortable moments, especially for anyone who suffered from vertigo. One nasty time my horse fell and rolled with me down a slope, till stopped by a tree just above a precipice. The instructor coldly commanded me to remount.'

Rodzianko later finished the senior course at Tor di Quinto in Rome. Before passing out he gave the party of his life at the Hotel Excelsior. At 6 am he found the last of his guests, including the entire staff of the cavalry school, solemnly fishing sardines from the grand piano which had somehow become filled with champagne!

He was soon to return to Russia, but first spent a month in Ireland visiting horse dealers on behalf of the Italian cavalry. This was a country he was one day to know well. In 1929 – with a world war and a revolution intervening – Rodzianko was to be invited to Dublin to train the Irish Army's jumping team.

Meanwhile, international horse shows had come into being. In 1906 Count Clarence von Rosen of Sweden proposed to the International Olympic Committee (IOC) at its congress in Athens that equestrian events should be included in the next Olympic Games. The proposal did not generate much enthusiasm; it was said they would be very expensive to stage and would probably not attract sufficient support. Nevertheless, following a suggestion by Baron Pierre de Coubertin, who had founded the IOC in 1894, von Rosen subsequently put forward proposals for three Olympic equestrian contests: dressage, a pentathlon, and a game called 'jeu de rose' – a form of mounted tag which was then enjoying considerable vogue on the continent.

Britain's first International Horse Show was held at Olympia, London, in June 1907 and was described as 'bursting into flower'. Massed banks of hydrangeas were everywhere. The presiding genius was Lord Lonsdale. Master of the Cottesmore Hounds, he was a

keen collector of chestnut horses with white legs, and was known as the 'Yellow Earl' because of his strong partiality for that colour – even his cars, carriages, liveries, stable rugs and buckets were all of a brilliant yellow hue.

At that inaugural show the jumps were brought into the arena at a half-speed gallop on a yellow dray drawn by chestnut carriage horses, ridden by postillions in yellow livery. The backdrop represented Lowther Castle, Lord Lonsdale's seat, and its surrounding park. The earl directed operations from the centre of the arena, an imposing figure in full evening dress with a silk hat and yellow buttonhole, and always a cigar. He loved ostentation and was prepared to pay for it; that first show was a dazzling display, but a financial flop.

Chargers, troop horses and hunters were all included, as well as harness horses in profusion. Most of the jumping contestants were cavalry officers, but there were already in existence several very talented civilian riders who exhibited their expertise at the local and county shows around the country. One of them was Fred Foster, the only Englishman to win at the first Olympia; Tommy Glencross and his almost equally famous brother, Jimmy; and W. V. Grange. Fred Foster owned Swank, the holder of the British High Jump record, who was ridden by Donald Beard to clear 7ft 6¼in at Olympia in 1937 – a record which still stands.

That first show was truly international, with entries from Belgium, Spain, Canada, France, Holland, Ireland and the USA. Prize money was £120 to the winner, £80 to the second, £60, £40, £30, £20, £10, and seven prizes of £5 each. Even in those days the prizes were well spread for the eleven competitions, which each attracted an entry of some seventy-five horses.

The fences were advanced for those days, but there was no time limit and circling before a fence, which now counts as a refusal, was permitted. Thus if a rider felt that his horse was approaching a fence on a wrong stride, and would take off either too far away or too close, he pulled him round in a circle and tried again. There were laths or slats on every fence and the horses had to jump super-cleanly, for the merest touch would send the slats floating to the ground. In outdoor contests, many arguments ensued as to whether it was the horse or the wind that had displaced them.

A top-hatted judge stood by each fence with notebook in hand and accompanied by a 'runner' in the shape of a small boy. When the round was completed, these small boys would be given their judges' slips and run with them to the judge who had the unenviable job of computing them on the rails.

At this first International Horse Show the British cavalry officers did not finish in the first dozen. Their interests lay in the direction of hunting, racing and polo, which were regarded as more robust and manly amusements. Nor did they realise just how much time and trouble were expended by their foreign counterparts in dressage, and schooling on the flat as well as over jumps.

Count Clarence von Rosen's proposals for the inclusion of equestrian events in the Olympic Games were accepted by the International Olympic Committee, and plans were made to inaugurate them in the London Olympics in 1908. Lord Lonsdale agreed to incorporate the contest in his second International Horse Show at Olympia if there was a minimum of twenty-four entries from six different countries, but there was such an overwhelming response, with eighty-eight entries from eight countries, that the equestrian Olympics were abandoned for the next four years, eventually taking place at Stockholm in 1912.

Representing Britain at Olympia in 1908 were a trio of cavalry officers, Lieutenants Malise Graham, Geoffrey Brooke and Malcolm (Peach) Borwick, who were determined that British riders should be able to compete on equal terms with foreign show jumpers; the three were destined to earn much honour and glory in the show ring.

International jumping took place at the National Horse Show in New York; Alfred G. Vanderbilt, its president, inviting riders from overseas to compete there in 1909. The highest fence was 4ft 3in, and the second competition went to Britain, represented by five army officers under Major J. G. Beresford.

In 1909 several major innovations were introduced at Olympia. Perhaps the most notable was the presentation by King Edward VII of a gold cup – the precursor of the Nations' Cup – for a competition between teams of three officers representing their country. The second was the imposition of a two-minute time limit for completing the course. The third was the introduction of the

standing international rules of the day, and the fourth the first appearance of the Daily Mail Cup, to be contested by the winners of earlier competitions in the form of a championship; the cup is still presented today for the individual championship.

The international rules were as follows:

Refusing or bolting at any one

fence – 1st	2 faults
2nd	3 faults
3rd	debarred (eliminated)
Fall of horse and/or rider	4 faults
Horse touches fence without knocking it down	$\frac{1}{2}$ fault
Horse upsets fence with fore limbs	4 faults
Horse upsets fence with hind limbs	2 faults

One of the main features at Olympia was the High Jump championship, now replaced by the Puissance. The conditions laid down that the judges would also consider the form, or style, of the horses as they negotiated the jump, and further decreed that if any prizewinner succeeded in beating the record height of the previous year, he would receive an extra £25. As the previous year's record height was stated as 7ft 2in the standard must have been very high indeed.

The King Edward VII Cup was won that first year by France, followed by Belgium in 1910; the next year it returned to France. The Connaught Gold Cup for British officers, including 'forces of overseas dominions', was first presented in 1911, being won for England by Lieutenant Geoffrey Brooke on a small black mare, 15·2½hh, called Alice. Bought in Ireland as a government charger, she won this cup twice, and also two events in New York and two in Chicago, besides being in the winning British team in each place. She was seriously wounded in France in 1917 and did not survive the war.

More and more officers were now taking up show jumping as a sport. Included in the 1910 entry were Lieutenant C. T. Walwyn and Captain J. H. Gibbon; both were to be consistent winners in later years, and 'Taffy' Walwyn, a founder member of the British Show Jumping Association, became its president after Lord Lonsdale.

In 1912 Colonel Rodzianko made his first appearance at the International Horse Show in London. Now ADC to General Bezobrazov, commander-in-chief of the Imperial Guard, who gave him leave to ride in Russia and abroad, Rodzianko also organised evening classes in the Chevalier Guards' riding school and prepared a number of officers for international competitions. Accompanied by two of his pupils, Captain d'Exé of the Cuirassier Guards and Captain Ivanenko, Rodzianko brought two horses from Russia, while a third, recommended by Captain Tappi, instructor at the Italian Cavalry School, was sent, unseen, from Italy. This horse, Jenga, arrived at Olympia half-an-hour before the King Edward VII Cup competition was due to start; there was just time for Rodzianko to saddle him and ride out into the arena. The night before the contest Rodzianko had dreamed of jumping round the arena, winning and going up to the royal box to receive the cup from King George V. The dream came true in every detail, and the excitement of the Russian grooms knew no bounds. 'They went mad with delight,' Rodzianko recalled, many years later. 'One of them, a huge man with a beard, to the amazement of the English, flung his arms around me and kissed me as we rode into the yard to be photographed.'

The following spring he bought a beautiful-looking Irish thoroughbred named Mac-Gillycuddy o' the Reeks – pronounced most diversely by Russian tongues. He had a reputation for running away, but with his new master he proved to be a marvel, with great intelligence allied to superb conformation; two months later he helped Russia to win the King's Cup at Olympia for the second time.

By now the British officers had started to take their show jumping seriously, and none more so than Geoffrey Brooke whose best horse was named – with an almost uncanny prophetic sense of the way competitive riding was to develop in the next fifty years – Combined Training. A brown 15·3hh gelding with a star, he won the Connaught Cup at Olympia in 1912. Combined Training went all through the war on active service, being wounded on two occasions. In 1914 he broke loose from the horse lines at Walverghem and galloped off towards the German lines. Miraculously avoiding capture, he found his way back to friendly territory, and eventually returned to England. At Olympia in 1921 he was the first British winner of the King George V Cup, and was in the first British team to win the Prince of Wales Cup. He died in 1931 aged thirty.

Colonel Rodzianko was invited by the American Horse Show Society to compete in New York in November 1913. Jenga and MacGillycuddy, after a stormy passage of three weeks' duration across the Atlantic, arrived in good shape to begin two weeks' training. But they soon began to deteriorate and show signs of distress, and by the time the show opened they could hardly stand. Rodzianko only dared to jump Jenga, who won a couple of prizes.

The fences of the day – all uprights without groundlines and vast wings to prevent a horse running out – progressed by trial and error to more sophisticated obstacles. The solid single pole, sometimes 5ft high in a jump-off, was one of the most challenging; this was to become obsolete after some riders on small horses were injured when the horse decided to duck underneath instead of jumping it. Then someone invented a labour-saving gorse fence which, when hit, would spring back into an upright position. In the experimental prototype the springs were thought to be too weak, and a more virile mechanism was substituted, with the result that when a horse hit it with his forelegs, his hindlegs became entangled. This type of fence was also abandoned after a year or so.

By 1914, quite a lot had been learned about the construction of fences, while the ranks of civilian riders had increased sufficiently for the competitions at Olympia to be divided into military and civilian sections. The Russians came to London and achieved their hat-trick of victories in the King Edward VII Cup, fielding Jenga, MacGillycuddy and Zorab. Back in Petrograd, the Chevalier Guards gave a dinner to celebrate the victory, presided over by the Grand Duke Michael, who ordered the King's Cup, in the centre of the table, to be filled with champagne. It held over two bottles. Paul Rodzianko, the hero of the hour, was naturally dismayed when the Grand Duke ordered him to stand up and drink it. He lifted the great cup to his lips and, dimly aware of the laughter and cheers of the other officers, began to drink. Before it was half empty he fell unconscious and his party ended, almost before it had begun.

Cavalry officers all over Europe then started to train for the Olympic Games, due to be held in Berlin, but early in August war was declared and the carefree life of fraternal sportsmanship among the equestrian nations came to a close.

2 Between the Wars

After the war, show jumping did not take long to get into its stride again. Its organisation was still haphazard, as was its system of judging, which varied from show to show and in many instances was farcical. Soon, however, the sport was set on a firmer footing within a framework of jumping rules.

In 1921, the Fédération Equestre Internationale (FEI), with its headquarters in Brussels, was formed to act as the official governing body for equestrian sport. All competing countries are represented through affiliation of their national federations, and the executive committee meets regularly to formulate policy, review the rules and regulations, and deal with complaints. As the parent body, the FEI is the final authority and is inflexible in the enforcement of its rules. An FEI judge, selected from the panel of judges, and a technical delegate are present at every international show.

A year later the British Show Jumping Association (BSJA) was set up by a number of enthusiasts under the leadership of 'Taffy' Walwyn, who was already making his name at Olympia and other shows with a famous horse called Stuck Again. The BSJA formed its own set of rules, based on those of the FEI, and set about improving and encouraging the sport. One of the first requisites was a panel of qualified judges; until this time, the judge had often been the local MFH. Soon every equestrian-minded country had its own governing body, affiliated to the FEI, whose founder-members were France, Sweden, Belgium, Denmark, Italy, Japan, Norway and the United States.

The first post-war Olympic Games were held in Antwerp in 1920. Britain and Switzerland were caught in the net of veterinary quarantine regulations, and the team show jumping event went to Sweden, with Belgium second and Italy third. Both gold and silver individual medals went to Italy – represented by Lieutenant Tomaso Lequio on Trebecco and Major Valerio on Cento – a triumph for Caprilli's *il Sistema*.

In Paris four years later the equestrian events followed the pattern which still prevails: Three-Day Event, dressage and show jumping. Seventeen nations took part, represented by 99 riders and 110 horses, competing under FEI rules. Sweden again won the team event, followed by Switzerland and Portugal. Italy's Lieutenant Lequio with Trebecco, the gold medallists in Antwerp, finished second behind Lieutenant Gemuseus of Switzerland riding the Irish mare Lucette. Much of the credit for this Swiss victory in the individual event went to their chef d'équipe, Colonel Haccius, who schooled his men and horses on a gravel surface because of the state of the going. The bronze medal went to Lieutenant Krolikiewicz of Poland on Picador; only $\frac{1}{2}$ fault behind was Britain's Captain Bowden-Smith on Rozzer.

In 1925 the Swiss army buyer, Colonel Ziegler, approached Judge William Evelyn Wylie, the moving spirit behind the Dublin Horse Show, and pointed out that Switzerland bought between 500 and 1,000 horses in Ireland every year. He added: 'There are now on the Continent serious rivals to this horse trade of yours. If my country and yours could jump in friendly rivalry at Ball's Bridge, it would give the Irish horse a chance to show himself in world competition, and doubtless the Irish Army would participate.'

Invitations were issued and the Aga Khan presented a magnificent gold trophy, first jumped for in 1926. It was won by the Swiss, which was perhaps only just, under Colonel Ernst Haccius. They won again in 1927 and for the third time in 1930, to take the Aga Khan Cup outright. By now Dublin was established as a permanent port of call for the European nations.

The sport played only a minor role in the United States until a show jumping stable was established at the US Cavalry School at Fort Riley, Kansas, in time to train a team for the Olympic Games of 1932 in Los Angeles. From then until the outbreak of war, the Americans had a good team comprising Harry F. Chamberlain, Sloan Doak, William Bradford, Earl F. Thomson, Franklin Wing and others. Among those determined to put the USA on the world of show jumping map was Fred Bontecou, a well-heeled young army officer. He was in the US Olympic team in Paris in 1924, and two years later brought two Canadian-bred horses, Ballymacshane and Little Canada, to Olympia; on the former, a big grey horse, he became the first American to win the George V Cup. With one lone compatriot, Major George on Morgan, Bontecou rode his two horses in the Prince of Wales Cup, the US team losing to the home side by only $\frac{1}{2}$ fault.

In the early 1920s, Colonel Malise Graham

and Broncho were probably the most successful combination. A bay gelding, 16·3hh Broncho had been Lord Allenby's charger and a shell very nearly ended his career in March 1918. Three years later he was in the first winning team for the Prince of Wales Cup.

Another horse which served all through the war before beginning a successful show jumping career was Sea Count, a 15·3hh bay gelding with an eelmark. In 1919 he was transferred to the 14th/20th Hussars and, ridden by Lieutenant Sturt, won competitions on the Rhine. After the King's Dragoon Guards took over in 1921, Captain W. H. Muir rode Sea Count and thus began a great partnership. When the captain died his horse was given to Colonel Joe Hume Dudgeon and, when twenty years old, Sea Count was in four winning teams for the Prince of Wales Cup, won the Duke of York's Cup at Richmond in 1928 for five years running and again in 1936, was twice second for the King George V Cup and was in the winning team for the Aga Khan Trophy in 1931.

Meanwhile the civilians were also going strong, chief among them the immortal Tommy Glencross, who started riding show jumpers at the age of eleven, in partnership with his brother Jim. After paying their entry fees at their first show, the boys had only twopence left; this was spent on a cup of tea and a bun, which they shared. In 1907 Tommy won the champion High Jump at Olympia on All Fours, setting up a record of 7ft 4in which stood for many years. When he came out of the ring, to an immense reception, he sold All Fours for £1,000 – an unheard-of price for a jumper in those days – and Lord Lonsdale gave him a diamond tie-pin to mark the occasion. During his career Tommy Glencross imported twenty-two 'walers' from Australia; these included most of his best horses, such as Tradesman and All Fours. He also bought horses in Cornwall, among them his second-best jumper, a mare called Blink Bonny. After a year of negotiations, she was obtained only on condition that she should return to Cornwall to finish her days when she grew too old to jump.

Glencross rated W. V. Grange's Desire to be the best round-the-course show jumper – as opposed to high jumper – of the day, but his opinion would not at one time have been shared by the owner, who, because the horse was so perverse, refused to pay for a box to take him to any more shows. Wilf White, his rider, consequently rode him 20 miles across Cheshire to the next show, where Desire jumped a clear round and won his class. During the next fifteen years he won all over the country and lived to the age of thirty-one.

Another old war-horse was Hunter Bunter, named after General Sir Hunter Weston, whose charger he had been. Among his many victories, he took the High Jump at Olympia in 1924, after which he was sold to America by his owner, Harold Field, of Chichester, one of the biggest dealers in the south of England. Then there was Frank Allison of Penrith, whose 15-hand brown mare Temptress was nearly blind in her offside eye, having sustained a whiplash injury in her early days when she ran one season in the coach from Keswick to Windermere. Three times champion at the Royal Highland, she also won at Olympia, and had a foal by Royal Letter at the age of twenty-seven.

Women have distinguished themselves in the hunting field for more than two centuries and show jumping did not long remain a male preserve. One of the earliest lady show jumping riders was Mrs Harry Buckland, of the first husband-and-wife partnership to represent England in international equestrian events, at Ostend in 1902. Harry Buckland himself cleared 7ft 2in to win the High Jump at Olympia in 1909, riding the half-hackney, Marmion. He wanted the height raised again, but Lord Lonsdale refused to allow it, saying: 'You have already won. What is the point of breaking your own record?' Buckland always felt that Marmion could have cleared 8ft 2in that night.

Mrs Philip Blackmore, whose husband was the first official course-builder to the BSJA, also competed at Olympia in the early days with considerable success. But it was Lady Wright, one of the most outstanding women riders of all time, who was the first woman to ride a clear round at Olympia. She was on her first show jumper, If Not, a liver chestnut gelding with a blaze, standing just under 14·1hh. By a hackney stallion out of a Welsh pony mare, If Not started life pulling a milk float, and was sent to Lady Wright because he refused to remain in his field. He was hot and wild when he arrived but could certainly jump, so she sent him to her sister with a light sulky, and asked her to drive and make a friend of him. When the horse came back next

The first-ever outright winner of the King George v Gold Cup – Col Jack Talbot-Ponsonby

spring he was friendly and confident. If Not won £1,100 in his first two seasons. At the Bath championship in 1928 when, before the third jump off, the wall was being raised a third time, Lady Wright sent in a protest to the judges: 'My pony is under 14·1.' This protest was ignored, and If Not went in and won.

In 1928, Lady Wright bought Toby, who started life in chains on a farm, and later pulled a barge. After winning the Bath and West Championship he cleared 7ft in the High Jump at Olympia to win the Casani Cup against riders of seven nations. A great water jumper, he cleared 26ft at Dorchester one year – quite a spread for a 15·3-hand cobby animal. Jimmy Brown, a liver chestnut standing 16·2hh, is the best remembered of Lady Wright's horses. She bought him after some hesitation, as she was unable, she says, to hold one side of him. Every bit imaginable was tried without success; she finally solved the problem by adding a pair of snaps to his snaffle just before he entered the ring. With Toby, Jimmy Brown won the pairs class at Olympia in 1935 and 1936. In 1937 he won the

Daily Mail Cup and cleared 7ft 4in to finish second to Swank in the High Jump – a particularly remarkable performance as, owing to an accident, Lady Wright was unable to school him for the High Jump and had to rely entirely on his gallant disposition.

In the 1930s a new generation of riders came to the fore, one of the first being Captain J. A. Talbot-Ponsonby, who achieved a hat-trick of victories in the King George V Cup with Chelsea (1930 and 1932) and Best Girl (1934); he thereafter re-presented the cup for perpetual competition. Only three riders in the long history of this trophy have succeeded in winning it outright – the others being Colonel Harry Llewellyn and David Broome.

Jack Talbot-Ponsonby, a great man and a tremendous personality, who was to have a marked effect upon British show jumping in years to come, became interested in show jumping, having hunted all his life, as an officer cadet at Sandhurst. He first competed at Olympia on Chelsea in 1928. Later he forged an excellent partnership with Kineton, a Warwickshire-bred horse who won him the Connaught Cup at Olympia in 1936 and then

3 World War II and after

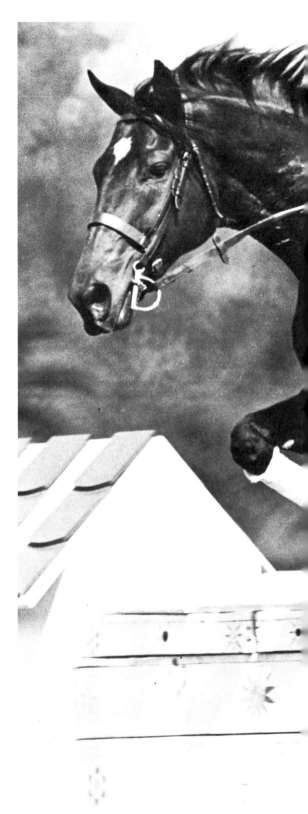

Pierre Jonquères d'Oriola: winner of two
individual gold medals for France, he rode Nagir
in the silver medal team at Mexico City in 1968

With the outbreak of war in September 1939 show jumping ground to a halt and its leading players were involved in the combat. Even Colonel Paul Rodzianko was back on active duty, attached to a pack-mule transport unit which, commanded by Colonel Joe Dudgeon, served in North Africa, Sicily and Italy. In a German prisoner-of-war camp at Spanenburg, Mike Ansell, Nat Kindersley and Bede Cameron retained their sanity by giving lectures to their fellows on the horse, hunting and show jumping. Colonel Ansell had already run a military horse show at Colchester in 1938, where the then-untravelled British civilians were astonished to find brightly coloured continental-type fences, already in vogue at the European military shows. After the war he was to plan Britain's advance to the top of the international show jumping tree, a campaign which necessitated several major changes in the conduct of the sport in England – the introduction of international rules and the abolition of the use of slats on fences, and thus the encouragement of a better class of horse, a higher standard of performance in the arena and a more arresting spectacle.

Soon after he was repatriated, Colonel Ansell was invited to be chairman of the BSJA and in 1944, nine months later, the first post-war national championship was staged at the White City. Tom Taylor, riding his brother Joe's Jorrocks, was favourite. A bay gelding, only 15·1hh, Jorrocks was already a big winner in 1939, when he was turned out to grass and not resaddled until 1945. After the war, he remained virtually unbeatable in the north, but in the national championship his chances were dashed when he stopped at the wall. With only one more horse to go, Ted Williams was lying first, second and third on Umbo, Huntsman and Leicester Lad, Umbo leading with ½ fault for displacing a slat. The last to jump was Colonel Nat Kindersley on Maguire, an eighteen-year-old chestnut gelding with a blaze and three white socks who had been a member of many successful British military teams. When Kindersley entered the arena he knew that it was a clear round or nothing. All went well until the white gate, which the old horse met on a wrong stride. When it seemed inevitable that he must either stop or hit it, Maguire gave a miraculous twist in mid-air, screwing his hindquarters safely over, and won the prize of the year amid great rejoicing. Just to prove

that it was no fluke, he won his second national title in three years at Newport, Monmouthshire.

In June 1946, at the White City, a three-day National Horse Show was held and, three months later, a Victory Show, the championship of which was won by a man destined to become one of the world's greatest and most successful international riders, Colonel Harry Llewellyn. Riding the big brown Irish horse Kilgeddin, by Toby Jug out of a mare by My Prince, he won the BSJA Victory Cup with two clear rounds. While still an undergraduate at Cambridge he had ridden Ego to finish second in the Grand National at Aintree.

Now show jumping was coming into its own again, even in Germany, where horse shows were held by officers serving with the BAOR; many of their horses had been captured with the cessation of hostilities. The National Horse Show in New York's Madison Square Garden was held again in 1945, and the International Olympic Committee met in Lausanne and decided to hold the Olympic Games in London in 1948.

In 1946 the FEI resumed its activities, and the French sent a team to Dublin to defeat Ireland and Sweden in the Aga Khan Trophy. France was the first team to dispense with the wholly military tradition of international riders. Travelling with them was one of the greatest riders of the post-war era, Pierre Jonquères d'Oriola, the only man to win two Olympic individual gold medals – in 1952 at Helsinki on Ali Baba, and at Tokyo in 1964 on Lutteur B. Riding a little Anglo-Arab mare called L'Historiette, he won the Grand Prix in Zurich – one of three international jumping shows held in Switzerland in 1946. With the Italian team was Lieutenant Piero d'Inzeo, the elder of the two illustrious brothers who are still winning top-class competitions today.

The following year Britain too broke with tradition and sent an all-civilian pioneer team to the international shows at Nice and Rome. Harry Llewellyn, Tom Brake, 'Curly' Beard, Bay Lane and Bobbie Hall did not exactly blaze a trail – indeed, in Nice it was said that, though the British had the best horses, they had no idea how to ride them. It was even suggested that they had better stick to bicycles – a remark rather hard to take. As Jorrocks so truly said, a man would sooner have imputations cast upon his morality than upon his horsemanship. The British civilians, denied the experience of international conditions with which the cavalry officers had come to grips before the war, had no knowledge of jumping at speed and were unaccustomed to the time element in jumping fences. Thus a jump-off against the clock was beyond them – they got as far as the barrage and no further. But, in Rome, Llewellyn and Kilgeddin won the Premio Campidoglio, the puissance, in which time is not decisive, and morale rose higher when 'Curly' Beard was runner-up for the Grand Prix on the little bay mare, Gay Lady.

Three months later the International Horse Show was reborn in all its glory – not at Olympia, but at the White City Stadium, where it settled down happily for twenty-one years. There was a good foreign entry including Ireland, France and Italy. France won the Prince of Wales Cup, with Britain as runner-up. The King George V Cup also went to France, represented by Pierre d'Oriola with Marquis III, a volatile little brown Anglo-Arab, whose owner said of him: 'Il a beaucoup de sang et beaucoup de coeur.'

British victories were scored by 'Curly' Beard on Eddie Broad's Monty in the Country Life Cup, by Bill Clarke on Paragon and by Brian Butler on the then unknown Tankard, a nine-year-old chestnut by Quart Pot out of Half Measure, who had run over fences without success. Now he was to win the Daily Mail Cup, the championship of the show – perhaps the biggest win of his career.

Paragon, who won the *Horse & Hound* Cup, was a brown gelding, probably Irish. He had arrived at Olympia with the Italian team in 1939. On the outbreak of war his owner, Count Pallistrelli, a cavalry officer, was recalled to Italy and, being unable to provide transport for the horse, left instructions that he was to be put down. These were not carried out and eventually the Italian horse found his way into the Cowfold, Sussex, stable of Tommy Grantham. When Bill Clarke, a former steeplechase jockey and later a show jumping rider of considerable repute, wanted a really quiet horse for an old gentleman to hack around the roads, Paragon was sent on trial. The horse was so lazy that he nearly fell over a matchbox. Clarke demanded of Tommy Grantham just what he meant by sending such an animal. 'Have you jumped the horse?' replied Grantham, unperturbed. 'Take him into your paddock and try him over a couple of fences. If you still don't like him, I'll take him back.'

Needless to say, Paragon was not sent back. After the war, when Count Pallistrelli returned to England he caught up with Bill Clarke and recognised Paragon as the horse he had ordered to be put down. To see a horse he had valued being jumped by another rider – especially of another nationality – cannot have been easy for him.

Britain's national show jumpers ride principally by instinct; not for them the theories and the finesse of Fillis and Caprilli. They are the 'naturals', some outstandingly good, more of them mediocre, depending on the strong arm to make up for what they lack in finesse. Yet these are the people who have made show jumping a peculiarly British institution. On the Continent the sport was considered to be 'très snob', the preserve of exclusive riding clubs and confined almost entirely to the rich. In Britain, the very reverse prevails. Very often those who show jump regularly are farmers or businessmen; while the professional classes are seldom represented. There have been show jumping greengrocers, butchers, shepherds, blacksmiths, horse dealers, ice cream manufacturers, bricklayers and even a hairdresser.

Several lady riders came to the fore in the early post-war years, among them Mrs 'Poppy' Townsend who rode an old army jumping mare, Big Sweep, in the 1940s. A chestnut by Galroy, foaled in 1926, Big Sweep was started upon her career by Jack Talbot-Ponsonby, who first won with her at the Royal Tournament. While jumping for the Prince of Wales Cup in 1937 she had cleared two fences when the band struck up the national anthem for the arrival of the Duke of York. In something of a quandary, her rider decided the only thing to do was to continue on around the course, which he did, touching his hat in the approved manner after completing a clear round. The judges, however, were somewhat put out. In 1948, ridden by Mrs Townsend for the third season running, Big Sweep won the Horse & Hound Cup at the White City.

The most outstanding lady newcomer to take the stage was Pat Smythe who was eighteen when, in 1947, she started competing at the White City on a little bay mare, barely 15hh, called Finality. The mare acquitted herself so well in London that Pat Smythe was invited to take her to compete with the British

Foxhunter, Col Harry Llewellyn's most famous partner

team in Ostend and Le Zoute in August. The other members of the team were Brian Butler's Tankard, Toby Robeson (Peter's father) with Rufus II, and Harry Llewellyn with Tal-y-Coed, Silver Fox and a novice horse called Foxhunter.

A rich bay gelding with black points, 16·3hh and foaled in 1941, Foxhunter came out at Newark in 1946. He won at Peterborough and Harry Llewellyn bought him in July. At the end of the season he went to Colonel Joe Dudgeon's place at Booterstown, Co Dublin, to learn to jump banks and get fit for the new season, which was the all-important Olympic year. In March Foxhunter was selected to train for the British Olympic team – less than a year after he jumped his first fence in public. On 14 August he represented his country in the Prix des Nations – a meteoric success story. Few second-season horses are selected to compete in the Olympic Games.

Among those who mustered at Aldershot for Olympic training under Colonel Joe Dudgeon were the three officers who had won Dublin's Aga Khan Trophy for Britain for the first time since 1931: Colonel Arthur Carr with Lucky Dip, Colonel Alec Scott with Notar and Colonel Henry Nicoll with Pepper Pot. Lucky Dip, a half-bred Hanoverian, was captured in a German veterinary hospital in 1945 by the 5th Royal Inniskillings. Notar, a Hanoverian-East Prussian crossbred horse had been a member of the German team in Dublin in 1939 and was captured by the 7th Armoured Brigade in May 1945 in the Wehrmacht veterinary hospital in Schleswig-Holstein. Pepper Pot, who won the International Trial at the Royal in 1947, was taken in Austria, by the 78th Division.

A vast number of horsemen from Germany and eastern Europe had surrendered to the 78th Division, including the German Cavalry Corps, who had marched back from Stalingrad, a Hungarian Corps and an assortment from the Black Sea and the Balkan States. Most picturesque of all was the White Russian Corps of Cossacks, who had been at war with Soviet Russia for the last twenty years, wandering round eastern Europe, living in tents and covered wagons, accompanied by their wives, their children and their horses. Nearly 50,000 horses from this great gathering were eating bare the valleys of Austria, and immediate steps had to be taken to disperse and dispose of them. Two hundred were taken by the British Army for recreational purposes, but many were in terrible condition. Among the last to be discovered was Pepper Pot, fractionally under 15·2hh with a lively eye and a jaunty step; only six years old and sound as a bell, his background and origin remained a mystery.

When the team was finally selected, it was led by Harry Llewellyn on Foxhunter, and comprised Colonel Henry Nicoll on Foxhunter's stable companion, Kilgeddin, and Colonel Arthur Carr on Monty.

The great day, 14 August, found fourteen nations coming under starter's orders at Wembley. The course-builder, Phil Blackmore, had worked all night to get the fences ready for the official inspection at 8.30 am. The ground was wet and badly poached here and there, adding to the difficulty of the course. Of the first twenty to start, eight were eliminated. The lead, with 8 faults, was held by the Chevalier Jean d'Orgeix of France with Sucre de Pomme. Henry Nicoll and Kilgeddin were round in 16. Monty got off to a bad start, stopping at the first fence and ultimately left

the ring with 35 faults. Only three teams succeeded in finishing intact; all the rest were eliminated. Foxhunter emulated Kilgeddin with 16 faults.

Finally, with only one to jump, Mexico's Reuben Uriza with Hatuey and Colonel F. F. Wing of the USA were level with d'Orgeix on Sucre de Pomme with 8 faults, the lowest score of the day. The last to go was the Mexican team captain, Colonel Humberto Mariles, a gifted and experienced horseman, riding a little one-eyed horse called Arete. Two from home and still clear, he landed squarely in the middle of the water and finally jumped the wall clear after a dead-right approach: 4 faults at the water, plus $2\frac{1}{4}$ for exceeding the time allowed, and the individual gold medal was safely within his grasp.

The Mexicans also won the team gold medals, with a score of $6\frac{1}{4}$, 8 and 20 faults (for Alberto Valdes on Chihuahua) to total $34\frac{1}{4}$. Spain was second on $56\frac{1}{2}$, represented by Colonel Morenes Navarro on Quorum, Commandant Gavilan y Ponce de Leon on Foregido and Commandant Jaime Garcia Cruz on Bizarro, with 20, $24\frac{1}{2}$ and 12 faults respectively. Britain, the only other team to finish, won the bronze medals of third place with 67 faults.

In the jump-off for the individual silver and bronze medals, a Mexican rider had the only clear round, while d'Orgeix with Sucre de Pomme was 1·2 secs faster than Franklin Wing on the American horse Democrat, each having a fence down. Sucre de Pomme, a bay Anglo-Arab, was hunted until he was six by his owner-breeder, Robert Peters, when d'Orgeix had the opportunity to jump a few fences on him and realised his potential; two months later he won the puissance in Paris, then the Grand Prix in Geneva and Ostend. In 1947 his successes included puissance competitions in Ostend and Paris, and in the Olympic year he took the coveted Rome Grand Prix and the same class in Paris. Democrat, a 15·3-hand brown thoroughbred gelding, won two classes at the National Horse Show in Madison Square Garden, New York, in 1940 and 1941, winning there again in 1946 and 1947 and also at the Royal Winter Fair in Toronto.

The Irish military team comprised Dan Corry on Tramore Bay, Fred Ahern on Aherlow and Jack Lewis on Lough Neagh – who eliminated his team in what was to be the end of the Irish pre-eminence. British ascend-

The jumping style of Major Raimondo d'Inzeo:
placed thirtieth when he made his Olympic debut
in 1948, he has since won both gold and silver
medals for Italy

ancy was already manifesting itself, as was that of the Italians. Raimondo d'Inzeo had made his Olympic debut in the Three-Day Event, in which he finished thirtieth individually, while in the show jumping his brother Piero was eliminated on Briacone.

The Mexican gold medallists returned home to a heroes' welcome, while the Americans – victors already in the Nations' Cup in Lucerne – scored again in the Prince of Wales Cup at the International Horse Show at the White City the following week and then crossed the Irish Sea to capture the Aga Khan Trophy in Dublin. Italy, France, Spain, Sweden and Turkey also competed at the White City. There were so many contestants for the King George V Gold Cup that the entries were split into three sections, with the first five in each one going through to the final. (This was the first and last time that women were eligible for this most coveted trophy, for in 1949 Princess Elizabeth presented her own cup for a ladies' championship.) Both Pat Smythe on Finality and Lulu Rochford on Ladybird V, a little bay Irish mare, only 15hh, and rather out of her class, went through to the final, when each was eliminated – Finality losing her rider at the double, three from home.

Franklin Wing had won the first section on his reserve Olympic horse, Totilla, a big brown gelding foaled in 1933; formerly owned by the Wehrmacht, he was captured by the US 3rd Army in 1945 during its advance through southern Germany. Almost certainly a pre-war jumper, he won in New York in 1947 and returned to Germany to win the Grand Prix at Aachen the following year.

Foxhunter won the second section, and the third went to another US combination, Captain Jim Russell on Rattler, also an Olympic reserve, bred in 1937 by a rancher in Texas. He won the puissance at Fort Riley, Kansas, in 1947, and after being selected as an Olympic 'possible' won in Lucerne and Aachen.

In the final, Foxhunter went clear and into the jump-off, when he had a brick out of the wall; but no one else could come within a fence of him, though Colonel Wing and Totilla were on level peggings until the very last fence. So Foxhunter, only seven years old, won his first King George V Cup, a trophy which he took again in 1950, then won outright three years later.

Harry Llewellyn considered himself too heavy to ride steeplechasing any more, but he had that spring brought off a sterling double at the National Hunt Festival at Cheltenham, winning the Foxhunters' 'Chase on State Control and the United Hunts 'Chase on his wife's Bay Marble. The addition of the King's Cup for show jumping provided a unique triple crown – a record most unlikely to be challenged.

There was still a long way to go before Britain took her first Olympic gold medals for show jumping at Helsinki, four years later. Major 'Ged' O'Dwyer, who was running a number of show jumping courses at this time, considered that British riders were divided between adopting the old Weedon style of riding and the new forward-seat style. 'Having a certain knowledge of both methods, they are at a loss as to when to apply one and when the other, instead of sticking to the new school of thought, now proved right over forty years – invented by Caprilli and the Italians, perfected before the war by other countries such as Germany, Ireland and France, and typified at its best by the Mexicans, who are super horsemen, always in complete and utter control – though some of their methods would not be countenanced by our standards.'

Tom Brake, a pioneer show jumper, commenting at the time on the future of British show jumping, admitted it was very difficult for his horses and himself to jump under FEI rules one day and BSJA the next. 'If we are going to keep on sending teams abroad and inviting foreign teams here to jump under FEI rules, we must ask the BSJA and local show organisers to adopt these rules . . . I am quite sure that this new mode of jumping will bring a better class of horse into the jumping game, and a more sporting crowd of jumping people.' He continued, 'If we consider ourselves to be among the best horsemen in the world, we must now practise, the only way that will let us get to the top. We have the best horses and riders – but we *must* have the practice.'

4 Into Europe

Colonel Mike Ansell meanwhile had his sights set accurately upon the reforms he had envisaged during his years in a prisoner-of-war camp. Soon, very few shows in England staged their jumping competitions under the old BSJA rules, which included the use of slats, 4 faults for a knockdown with the forelegs and 2 faults for hitting a fence with the hindlegs. In the switch-over to FEI, courses became more colourful, varied and ambitious. The speed element was introduced increasingly into competitions, and almost every jump-off took place against the clock.

Realising, too, that competition abroad was absolutely vital to any international effort, Mike Ansell saw to it that the most promising international riders were included in teams for the Continent as often as possible. In Paris, in November 1948, Mrs 'Pug' Whitehead with the straight-necked bay Niblick, Mary Whitehead with Nobbler, 'Ruby' Holland-Martin with High Jinks and Tal-y-Coed, and Harry Llewellyn with Monty and Foxhunter took on the best from France, Italy, Spain, Switzerland and Belgium. Monty won two competitions and his rider was the highest classified in the show, with Piero d'Inzeo runner-up.

Plans to send a British team to New York and Toronto had to be abandoned for lack of funds and, with the United States military team disbanded after the Olympic Games, Mexico swept the board, winning the New York Nations' Cup for the third year running, with the French as runners-up on their first visit in twelve years. In Toronto it was much the same story, though the French won the Nations' Cup for the first time since 1927.

A new British team member at the Palais des Sports show in Paris in April 1949 was the Countess of Dudley, now the Dowager Duchess of Marlborough. She was an enthusiastic pupil of Colonel Rodzianko who had started coaching again while in BAOR. When asked how she was progressing, her tutor shrugged, then admitted: 'She may not make the top grade, but she is very brave – and she smells divine!'

Later in the same year, in London, Major Douglas Stewart on Kilgeddin, Harry Llewellyn on Foxhunter, Wilf White on Phil Oliver's Talisman and Brian Butler on Tankard won the Prince of Wales Cup for the first time since the war, while Brian Butler on Tankard won the King George V Cup. It must be admitted that the French had

The 'full-back' of the British team in 1952 and 1956 – Wilf White with Nizefela

only a scratch team, the Dutch and the Belgians were not very strong and the Irish were fielding young horses, but Ireland did win the Aga Khan Trophy in Dublin soon afterwards.

The last shows in August 1949 were at Ostend and Le Zoute. Peter Robeson, then aged seventeen, represented Britain on Rufus, who had undergone Olympic training, and Craven A, who was destined to make a great name and is still going strong. A brown mare bred in 1942, she won the puissance at Ostend at 6ft 3in, beating Marquis III, and in Paris soon afterwards was second in the European Grand Prix. The other significant newcomer to the team was Wilf White, the Cheshire rider who had enjoyed so much success in pre-war days on Desire. Now he was riding his own horse, Nizefela, who was to become the cornerstone of the British team and was described by Harry Llewellyn as: 'Steady as a rock, jumping clean and big with (to the foreigners) nerve-shattering regularity. There is no better Nations' Cup horse in the world.' By a shire stallion out of a mare who was nearly clean bred, Nizefela pulled a plough in his early days. Wilf White paid £100 for him and upgraded him in only seven shows. His first foreign tour was to Nice and Rome in 1949, and this enormously powerful horse with his characteristic of kicking back at his fences was in the first British team ever to win a Nations' Cup on the Continent – in Geneva at the end of the season, with France and Italy as runners-up. Earlier, at the White City, he had lost the King George V Cup by ¾ of a time fault.

Also in 1949, the first Horse of the Year Show was held at the Harringay Arena in north London. Captain Tony Collings, a well-known West Country figure in hunting, polo and showing circles, had the idea of staging a championship show at the end of the season for all categories of horse and pony, and Mike Ansell thought it an excellent scheme. This indoor show, run by the BSJA, included showing classes in addition to the jumpers, and from the outset was a great success with exhibitors and the public.

Riders from Belgium, France and Ireland came to that first Harringay meeting. Among the Irish team were Iris Kellett with Rusty, Captain Ian Dudgeon with Go Lightly, and the ace steeplechase jockey, Tim Hyde from Co Tipperary, with the outstanding novice horse in Ireland that season – Mrs McDowell's Hack On. Iris Kellett bought the great Rusty in 1946. During the war his breeder, Mr Ring, had used him in the plough six days a week, hunting him on Sundays. In 1948 he beat all the crack horses in the international championship in Dublin, and in 1949 won the newly incepted Princess Elizabeth Cup at the White City, which he retained in 1950. Miss Kellett broke her leg very badly in the spring of 1952 and nearly died of tetanus, but she was winning again two years later.

Tim Hyde, perhaps best known for his partnership with the mighty Prince Regent, was a consummate horseman and a wholly delightful character. He won many top-class competitions on Hack On, but sadly broke his back when a young horse fell with him over the double bank at Clonakilty show. He spent the rest of his life in a wheel chair, which had its permanent billet on the rails in the Jumping Pocket throughout the Dublin shows. Hack On, later ridden with equal success by Colonel Jack Lewis, formerly of the Irish Army team, was a natural jumper, who made his talent known in his youth by persistently jumping a solid 6ft demesne wall surrounding the estate in Cork where he was bred.

Ian Dudgeon's Go Lightly was the most successful, internationally, of all the horses jumping in Ireland from 1950 onwards. A bay gelding, 16·0hh, he was a headstrong, difficult horse, who won the Daily Telegraph Cup at Harringay in 1953 and again in 1954. It was in Dublin that he really shone, however, winning the civilian and the international championship in 1950 and 1952, and the civilian championship in 1951; in 1954 dividing it with Rusty, and in 1959 sharing it with Tommy Wade and Dundrum after jumping off four times – the last over two straight fences at 6ft 1in. He was then seventeen years of age. It is of interest that in 1956 the international championship in Dublin – and in 1957 the civilian title – went to Ian's father, Colonel Dudgeon, with his twenty-three year old grey mare Seaspray – their combined ages totalling a hundred years. Both father and son had injuries to the knee – a very vital joint when riding a horse. Ian was wounded in the knee during the war; the Colonel shattered one of his kneecaps on the upright of the water jump at Ball's Bridge.

Iris Kellet and Rusty went well indeed to beat Foxhunter for the Diana Stakes, while the first-ever 'Show Jumper of the Year' title went to Pat Smythe on Finality, who by now had changed hands twice – sold first to Tommy Makin, and then to Jimmy Snodgrass from Scotland.

In 1950 the United States Equestrian Team was formed. Its first captain was Colonel John Wofford, whose three sons John, Warren and Jimmy all later became Olympic riders. Wofford was succeeded by Arthur McCashin. In 1937 and 1938 civilians were permitted to ride against military teams for the Irish Free State Challenge Trophy in New York. McCashin, riding a team of three horses – Will Gallop, Greyflight and Bayflight – for the late Julian Bliss, was the 1937 winner with a total of only 1½ faults. The competition was judged under American Horse Show rules which penalise a horse for touching a fence. In 1938, with the same team except that Modernistic replaced Bayflight, all three horses jumped clear rounds and had to jump off with the Chilean team. Eventually they won with only ½ fault over six rounds. On the outbreak of war McCashin gave up jumping to become a flier.

Alan Oliver, whose 'spaceman' technique may
have cost him a place in the 1952 Olympic team

In 1950, upon the mechanisation of the
US Cavalry, he responded to a call for civilian
riders to fill the gap. Born in Ireland, where
he is still a frequent visitor and has horses in
training, he started show jumping at the age
of eight with two Irish ponies, both of which
jumped large heights for their size.

In the same year German teams also began
to appear at international shows for the first
time since the war, laying the foundation for
the formidable collection of Olympic gold
medals they were to win in later years. At
this time Britain won the Nations' Cup in
Lucerne, London and Dublin, and came
second to the home side in Nice. In the
autumn the British team went on the North
American fall circuit, to lose the Nations'
Cup in Harrisburg to the Mexicans, but to
win in Toronto. The individual heroes of this
expeditionary force were Wilf White and
Nizefela, who won two competitions in Harrisburg and three in Toronto, dividing two more.
Foxhunter won three competitions, while
Peter Robeson and Craven A were also
winners in Harrisburg, beating Mexico's
Olympic gold medallists, Colonel Mariles
with Arete, after no fewer than four barrages.

The pre-Olympic year of 1951 was one of
great activity, Britain being represented in
eight Nations' Cups and winning in London,
Dublin and Rotterdam. This was the year
in which Alan Oliver first joined the British
team. He was selected when he was aged
nineteen to ride in the Prince of Wales Cup at
the White City with Red Star II. On Nations'
Cup day his father, Phil, told me with justifi-

able pride that Alan had already cut a field of hay before leaving home that morning. Having helped to win the Prince of Wales Cup for his country, he eventually became the leading rider of the year in England.

Another significant newcomer to the team was Colonel Duggie Stewart, who in 1948 had been a member of the British Olympic Three-Day Event team. On the big German-bred Bones he helped to win the first Nations' Cup in which he competed, and had automatically staked a claim for the scrutiny of the selectors.

Training for the short list commenced in February with horses going into work for the long conditioning period. Harry Llewellyn and Wilf White, both already a certainty for the Olympic team, were invited with Colonel Stewart, Alan Oliver and Peter Robeson to train under Colonel Jack Talbot-Ponsonby. The horses were Foxhunter, Nizefela, Aherlow (a brown Irish mare, loaned by 'Ruby' Holland-Martin), Nobbler, Red Star, Phil Oliver's Talisman and Pat Smythe's Prince Hal. As women were not yet eligible to ride in the Olympic Games Miss Smythe loaned this former indifferent racehorse – a chestnut by Hallowmas out of Morna by My Prince – who was destined to become one of the most successful show jumpers in the world.

Colonel Stewart, commanding the Royal Scots Greys in Germany, had little time to school, but after a final try-out at Aldershot it was decided he was a better bet than either Alan Oliver, whose horses were not quite of Olympic standard, or Peter Robeson, who became reserve for the team. Oliver's style too went against him. He had from the age of eleven, when he started riding his father's horses in open competitions, adopted the 'spaceman' technique: in mid-air, his hands on the reins and his feet in the irons were often his sole physical contact with his horse. Nevertheless, he was Britain's leading national rider in 1951, 1953 and 1954, and runner-up in 1952 and 1955. Paul Rodzianko, who could be more critical than anyone when occasion demanded, was strangely tolerant of Alan's acrobatics: 'He rides, and *wins*, which is the acid test, in the style which suits him best.'

The Nations' Cup victory by the Argentine riders in Lucerne had provided the first guideline to South American form. In 1950, at the first Pan-American Games, held in Buenos Aires, Chile was the winner with 40 faults in hand from the Argentine, with Mexico and Brazil filling the remaining places. Chile had the advantage of possessing a flourishing cavalry, with well-equipped schools in Quillota and Santiago, and still holds the international High Jump record. This was set up in 1949 by Captain Alberto Larraguibel Morales on Huaso; having cleared 8ft 1½in, the horse lived out his days in honourable retirement. In 1950, Captain Morales won the individual competition on Julepe from the crack Argentinian, Colonel Carlos Delia, on El Linyera, with two other Chilean riders tying for third place – Joaquim Larrain on Pillan and Ricardo Echeverria on Bambi.

The Americans were determined to make a good showing in the 1952 Olympic Games in Helsinki. The team finally selected consisted of Arthur McCashin on the grey Miss Budweiser, Bill Steinkraus on Colonel Wofford's Hollandia, and Colonel John Russell with the famous Democrat. Miss Budweiser, a seven-year-old 16·2-hand mare, had been loaned to the team by Mrs Carol Durand, America's top lady rider at that time, who like Pat Smythe was ineligible to ride in the Olympics.

Bill Steinkraus too was a highly experienced show jumping rider, graduating to the US team as the first product of the equitation events which culminate in the ASPCA Championships each year during the fall circuit. He has always been the sort of quiet, efficient, natural horseman who stands out in a competition, win or lose. Helsinki, 1952, was only the start of a brilliant international career when, on Hollandia, a son of the good jumping sire Bon Nuit, he helped the US team to win the bronze medals.

Sixteen teams arrived in Helsinki – the British, greatly daring, having travelled by air – and inspected the course of thirteen fences (nineteen jumps, with the combinations) an hour before the 8 am start. Colonel Stewart and Aherlow kicked off for Britain with a respectable 12 faults, all three mistakes coming at parallels. Then Nizefela and Wilf White were clear until the final gate, for 4 faults. With Foxhunter still to come, the position looked rosy for Britain, lying second on 16 to Italy's 12. For the Italians, Piero d'Inzeo had still to start; Uruguay, his French-bred chestnut, a considerable performer over puissance fences, was a worthy opponent for

Foxhunter. But d'Inzeo, involved in controversy with an official, missed his turn and was eliminated by the jury. Then Foxhunter, spooking at the fences, set off without nearly enough impulsion, climbed over the first four, hit the planks, just got away with it at the double and then threw himself over the wall, almost from a standstill, to stop at the bank of flowers with his rider hanging round his neck. Somehow, with his spur caught in the girth, Llewellyn managed to get back into the saddle. Foxhunter hit the bank and flowers, flipped over the water, hit the gate and jumped the last fence clear, to total $16\frac{3}{4}$ with time penalties.

The USA were now in the lead with 23 faults, followed by Portugal (24), the Argentine (28), Brazil ($28\frac{1}{2}$), Germany (32), Britain ($32\frac{3}{4}$), Spain (35), and France, Sweden and Mexico disputing eighth place with 36. The individual lead was held by Fritz Thiedemann on Meteor for Germany, with the only clear round.

During the interval between the two rounds, Jack Talbot-Ponsonby gave Foxhunter an hour's work and Harry Llewellyn had an hour's sleep. By 3.15 the stadium was packed and soon the Argentine was out of the reckoning when the team's first horse went lame. Duggie Stewart was round in 4 on Aherlow, and Wilf White and Nizefela were clear except for a highly controversial fault at the water. Then came Foxhunter, his old, settled, reliable self again, to achieve a clear round and give victory to his team.

Chile finished second, five faults ahead of Britain's score of $40\frac{3}{4}$. The United States came third with 52·25 faults, and Germany sixth with 60, behind Brazil and France. The Mexicans, defending champions, had shot their bolt and were lying ninth.

In the jump-off for the individual medals were d'Oriola on Ali Baba for France, Chile's Oscar Cristi on Bambi, Wilf White on Nizefela, de Menezes of Brazil on Bigua, and Fritz Thiedemann on Meteor. Ali Baba, who went first in the jump-off, was clear to win in 40 secs with the only clear round; Bambi had 4 in 44, and Meteor had two down in achieving the best time, 38·5 secs. Bigua had two down and Nizefela, who was not at his best against the clock, hit three.

The British team's horses, showing the effects of their great effort at Helsinki, did not figure prominently among the prizewinners at the 1952 International Horse Show. The King George V Cup went to Spain, represented by the ebullient nineteen-year-old Carlos Figueroa on Gracieux, a little chestnut French-bred Anglo-Arab. The Spaniard was so delighted by his victory that he embraced in turn his horse, his groom, and finally his opponent in the barrage – Harry Llewellyn, who was riding The Monarch at this time.

The Monarch, a big brown gelding foaled in 1940 in Kilkeel, helped to win the 1951 Nations' Cups in Dublin and Rotterdam, after which he was bought by that great supporter of show jumping, the late Robert Hanson, for his son Bill. In 1953, Bill and The Monarch became the first British combination ever to win the Grand Prix in Rome – from the Count di Medici on Fortunello – and also won on the North American circuit. Then, in 1954, Bill Hanson suffered a fatal illness at the tragically young age of twenty-nine.

The leading combination of 1952 on the home front was Pat Smythe and the grey mare Tosca, who also headed the list in 1953. Foaled in 1945, Tosca was bought out of Ireland in a draft of horses by Phil Oliver and sold very cheaply as she was headstrong and temperamental. But a season's hunting in Gloucestershire settled her down, and after coming out in 1951 she never looked back, winning top prizes all over the country, though she did not do well abroad.

In 1952 the FEI started the Junior European Team Championship to encourage and bring on the young entry aged fourteen to eighteen years. The first running, in Ostend, was won by Italy with the assistance of Graziano Mancinelli, destined to win the European title in 1961 and the Olympic individual gold medal in Munich eleven years later. In 1954, in Rotterdam, the German junior team who finished second included two future senior internationals – Hermann Schridde, who won the men's European title in 1965, and Alwin Schockemohle, second for this title on three occasions.

Another, even more successful, German rider, Hans Günter Winkler, first appeared in 1952 and first won the World Championship only two years later. The year when Britain won her only team gold medals for show jumping thus saw the beginnings of future German supremacy in the ring.

5 Helsinki to Rome 1953~1959

The next step forward for show jumping was the setting up, in 1953, of a World Show Jumping Championship. Organised by the FEI, it was initiated in Paris and run under a new formula, with three qualifying competitions and a final in which the four top-placed riders at this stage changed horses. It has been argued that this proves very little; the system does, however, produce a fascinating comparison of horsemanship, and rarely throws up a false winner.

The four finalists in that first World Championship – which at the start was an annual event but is now held every four years, gaining in status accordingly – finished in this order: Francisco Goyoaga of Spain riding Quorum, Fritz Thiedemann of West Germany on Diamant, Pierre Jonquères d'Oriola of France on the Olympic gold medallist, Ali Baba, and Piero d'Inzeo of Italy on Uruguay. 'Paco' Goyoaga, who won by the narrow margin of $\frac{1}{2}$ fault with a total of 8, was the leading Spanish rider at this time, while his uncle, Colonel Jaime Garcia-Cruz, and his army team contemporaries began to be eclipsed.

At the 1953 International Horse Show, Harry Llewellyn and Foxhunter completed their hat-trick of victories in the King George V Gold Cup. It was a very wet year, and some 50 tons of sand were required as mopping-up material before the course was deemed to be ridable. With three initial clear rounds from Ireland – including the young Captain Michael Tubridy on Red Castle – Foxhunter's chief and most dangerous rival appeared to be the brilliant Italian-bred Merano ridden by Raimondo d'Inzeo. But Merano brushed a section of coping from the wall, and it was Red Castle who took Foxhunter to a second barrage before going under.

This was Foxhunter's last outstanding victory, though he went on jumping, and won his seventy-eighth and last international competition at Dublin in 1956. He had already earned his niche in the annals of the great, and for a few years more his public were privileged to see him when he made an annual journey to the Horse of the Year Show to 'present' his trophy to the winner of the Daily Express National Foxhunter Championship – a very moving occasion.

Micky Tubridy, the most promising of all Paul Rodzianko's new crop of Irish Army riders, went on to win the international championship in Dublin on the discovery of the year, the bay Ballynonty. Tubridy left the army that winter. The following spring he was found unconscious in a field after an accident with a young horse and died on the way to hospital. A great horseman, one of the few post-war riders to approach the class of the pre-war stars, and a most delightful and unassuming personality, he was especially popular in the United States, his widow being invited to the National Horse Show in New York, as guest of the committee, for several years after.

Raimondo d'Inzeo and Merano turned the tables on Foxhunter in the 1953 Daily Mail Cup. Merano, a 16-hand bay gelding, was bought by d'Inzeo in 1950 for only £200. Merano's breeder had seen him jump a gate as a yearling and preferred him to go to a great rider, and be given every opportunity, than be sold for more money to an inferior rider. At the end of 1953 d'Inzeo sold him for £4,000 to Sandrino Perrone, well-known sportsman and editor of Italy's leading daily newspaper, but they were not suited to one another – Perrone could not hold the horse in

'Paco' Goyoaga, the first World Champion, here on the German mare Toscanella

35

a snaffle, and Merano went kindly in no other bit. He was then bought by the Italian Federation for £3,000 and returned to Raimondo d'Inzeo for international competitions.

The West German riders really came to the fore in 1954. In Madrid, Hans Günter Winkler won the first of his two consecutive world titles at the expense of d'Oriola with Arlequin D; Goyoaga, the holder, on the Olympic horse Quoniam, and Salvatore Oppes of Italy on Pagoro. This year, for the only time in the history of the championship, the holder was immediately eligible for the final without previous qualification. Winkler had only two years of international experience behind him but was exceptionally gifted. He won the title riding Halla, another horse whose name will live on in show jumping history. A ten-year-old brown mare, she was by the trotter Oberst out of a half-bred mare called Helene, but she was almost thoroughbred in appearance, in startling contrast to the traditional German jumpers of that time, who were principally heavy Holsteins. After her title win she went to the United States and Canada and was remarkable for her consistency, winning the High Jump and the championship in Harrisburg – Germany's first victories in the US for over twenty years – and four of the biggest competitions in New York.

In 1955, on their native heath at Aachen, Winkler and Halla retained their world title after an epic battle with Raimondo d'Inzeo riding his brother Piero's horse, Nadir. In third place was a British officer from BAOR, Major Ronnie Dallas, on the huge German horse Bones. Two weeks later, Halla won the gruelling Hamburg Jumping Derby for the first time.

Germany's growing supremacy in 1954 was underlined by Fritz Thiedemann, a great precision rider who invariably rode massive Holstein horses. On Meteor, a 16·3hh bay gelding, he won the King George V Gold Cup after a hard duel with Alan Oliver on Red Admiral, and went on to win the *Country Life and Riding* Cup at the same show. Then Thiedemann went to the United States to win the international championship in New York, and to lose that in Toronto by a narrow margin. A year later he attained the Grand Prix in Aachen, among eighteen other international victories, and in 1956 won twenty-four international classes and was in the winning German Olympic team.

Thiedemann had a wide choice of mounts among the fifty show jumpers at the Holstein stud at Elmshorn, where the breeders have their own club of 4,000 members, and 2,500 registered mares. The aim is to produce clean-limbed, big-boned, warm-blooded horses with a long stride, conforming to a standardised type. In recent years, with the emphasis on riding rather than driving, the breed has been improved from within by thoroughbred blood.

Major Paul Stecken, a former German cavalry officer, attributes the success of the German show jumpers not so much to their innate ability, formidable though it is, but to the system under which they are trained. Of ten German horses, taken at random, he considered that eight would be good jumpers due to the dressage they receive from the time they are first broken. In a big German national competition there are often 100-per-cent clear rounds. The horses have impeccable manners and are under absolute control by their riders. Being possessed of an unusually equable temperament, they are far easier to ride than a thoroughbred animal. Hans Winkler, however, has always favoured the quality horse, and his influence among the younger riders has brought a different type of animal into the German team of today, which is still at the top of the Olympic tree.

In 1955, another pre-Olympic year, the United States team made its first appearance at the Pan-American Games, held in Mexico City. It was not an auspicious initiation as they finished fourth of four nations. Over a tough course, Mexico, the winners, knocked up $71\frac{1}{4}$ faults, but held at bay both the Argentine ($89\frac{3}{4}$) and Chile ($122\frac{1}{2}$).

The balance of power had now shifted drastically. Britain did not win a single Nations' Cup that season. The Italians captured the Prince of Wales Cup (which Britain lost for the first time for seven years), the Aga Khan Trophy and the Nations' Cup in Paris. The Germans beat the Italians in Aachen. It was a difficult interregnum for Britain with Foxhunter retired, Pat Smythe's Prince Hal and Peter Robeson's Craven A past their best, and only Wilf White and Nizefela still on the active list of the top combinations of horses and riders. Yet several top-flighters were also emerging, outstanding among them being Dawn Palethorpe, now Mrs Warren Wofford. Her sister, Jill, who won the Princess Elizabeth Cup on Silver Cloud in 1950 when she was

Hans Winkler on Halla after winning the World Championship at Madrid in 1955

only seventeen, first produced the brown Irish horse Earlsrath Rambler, and rode him for two seasons. In 1954, when Dawn took him over, he won the Ladies' National Championship and the Leading Show Jumper title. A year later he scored the first of two consecutive victories in the Queen Elizabeth Cup, and was the first British reserve Olympic horse in 1956.

Selecting the British Olympic team – with the exception of Nizefela who virtually selected himself – was no easy task. Wilf White's two eventual team-mates were the two most experienced riders among the possibles: Pat Smythe on Robert Hanson's Flanagan, and Peter Robeson on the Hon

Dorothy Paget's bay gelding, Scorchin'. Flanagan, a chestnut gelding of Irish descent, was bought by Robert Hanson for his son Bill, who was never well enough to ride him. He was then given to Pat Smythe, who took him to the top. Flanagan made up for a certain lack of quality by being supremely genuine. In 1955 he won three classes in Paris, two at the White City and the Ladies' National Championship. The following year he won the Grand Prix Militaire in Lucerne before competing in the Olympics.

The 1956 Olympic Games were held in Melbourne, Australia, but because of a ban on the importation of horses the equestrian

Pat Smythe with Flanagan, a horse on which this
most famous of lady riders had great success

events took place in Stockholm. There was a field of twenty-three nations for the show jumping, which West Germany, represented by Fritz Thiedemann's Meteor, Hans Winkler's Halla and Alfons Lütke-Westhues's Ala, won with 40 faults. Italy – with Piero d'Inzeo on Uruguay, Raimondo d'Inzeo on Merano and Salvatore Oppes on Pagoro – was runner-up with 66. Only 3 points behind for the bronze medals were the British trio, 30 points clear of the Argentine, with the USA in fifth place.

Competing for the individual title Winkler had the misfortune to pull his riding muscle when Halla stood off too far at the penultimate narrow upright. In agonising pain, Winkler had to be carried from the stand and man-handled into the saddle for the second round. He was powerless to ride Halla, but simply pointed her the way she should go and the gallant mare did the rest, achieving the first clear round of the competition and, with a total of 4 faults, winning the gold medal. Raimondo d'Inzeo and Merano jumped the only other clear round; with two down and 8 faults in the first circuit, he won the silver medal. Piero d'Inzeo and Uruguay had two down and a stop for the bronze, and fourth place with 12 was divided between Thiede-mann on Meteor and Wilf White's Nizefela.

The following week there was an official international horse show in Stockholm and most of the teams stayed on to compete. Reinforced by the Olympic reserve combina-tion of Dawn Palethorpe and Earlsrath Rambler, Britiain won the jump-off for first place in the Nations' Cup and took home the King of Sweden's trophy. That year Britain won five of the six Nations' Cups in which she started – at Lucerne, in a field of eight; at Stockholm; in London and Dublin with four rival teams at each fixture, and in Rotterdam, again with four opponents. In Aachen, with a team including Nelson Pessoa, Brazil won her first European Nations' Cup.

The injury which Hans Winkler had sustained in the Olympic arena prevented him from defending the men's world title. Despite the presence of teams from the United States, South America and the Middle East, three of the four finalists were from Europe: 'Paco' Goyoaga on Fahnenkönig, Raimondo d'Inzeo with Merano, and Thiedemann on Meteor. The fourth was the Argentinian, Colonel Carlos Delia, with the chestnut Discutido, but

Ted Williams, a master of his trade, on the outstandingly successful Pegasus

their chances went by the board. D'Inzeo had $\frac{1}{2}$ fault for exceeding the time allowed on Merano, while Goyoaga and Thiedemann were clear.

Changing horses, Goyoaga on Merano had a stop at the parallels; d'Inzeo achieved a clear on Meteor, and Thiedemann hit the parallels on Fahnenkönig. Both Goyoaga and Thiedemann were clear in the last round, and d'Inzeo rode a precision round on Fahnenkönig. With $1\frac{1}{4}$ time faults, to total $1\frac{3}{4}$, he won the world title with $1\frac{1}{4}$ faults in hand from Goyoaga, in what was certainly a blanket finish.

In 1956 for the first time Britain fielded a team in the Junior European Championships, held in Spa, Belgium. Represented by Jan White, Mary Barnes, Michael Freer and Chris Middleton, Britain won the title and thereafter every Junior European Championship until 1961.

From Stockholm, the young American Olympic team went on to London for the International Horse Show. Trained by the former Hungarian cavalry officer, Count Bertalan de Nemethy, Frank Chapot, Hugh Wiley and, most of all, Bill Steinkraus received great admiration for their style of riding and the calm, smooth going of their quality horses. Steinkraus achieved the only two clear rounds in the King George V Cup, with his own horse Night Owl and Miss Joan Magid's First Boy, and nominated the latter as the winner.

During the winter, Ted Williams, who had started his long career riding for a horse dealer, was given his amateur licence. He was thus eligible for all official competitions under FEI rules, with the sole exception of the Olympic Games – from which riders who have at any time been professionals are permanently banned. Ted rode with the team for the first time in Nice and Rome. At Nice, the most successful British combination was Dawn Palethorpe and Earlsrath Rambler, who won the puissance at 6ft 6½in. In Rome, Ted Williams with the Australian Olympic mare Dumbell, Tom Barnes on Sudden, Dawn Palethorpe on Rambler, and the captain, Harry Llewellyn, on Aherlow were runners-up to Italy for the team event, with $42\frac{3}{4}$ faults to 16, followed by France, Portugal, Ireland and Holland.

In London, Rambler, Flanagan, Dumbell and Nizefela won back the Prince of Wales Cup from Italy. In Dublin, France won from Germany and Italy, with Britain fourth, the score being very close: 11, 12, 16 and $16\frac{3}{4}$ faults. Le Zoute saw Britain finishing fourth again, behind Switzerland, Holland and Belgium, but in Rotterdam the British reputation was retrieved in a victory over West Germany by $11\frac{3}{4}$ faults to 12. This success was largely due to another newcomer to the team, Ted Edgar, who jumped two clear rounds on his little chestnut mare, Jane Summers. Only 15·1hh, foaled in 1947, she was saved from the knacker's bullet for £5.

At the end of the 1956 season in Europe, Pat Smythe, Dawn Palethorpe and Ted Williams went on the North American tour. There Ted Williams and Pegasus – the famous 15·1hh grey who was leading national horse from 1955 to 1958 – covered themselves with glory by winning the individual championships at all three shows – Harrisburg, New York and Toronto. In competition with teams from the USA, Canada, Mexico, Chile, the Argentine and Ireland, the British trio had a slight edge on the Americans, with twelve outright wins apiece but more high placings down the list.

In 1957, following the reasonable suggestion put forward by the South American nations that the title 'World Championship' should only be given to an event which also included entries from the western hemisphere, this was renamed the European Championship. Hans Winkler, defending his title at Rotterdam, rode a chestnut half-brother to Halla with a very different temperament, called Sonnenglanz. This horse played a leading part in Winkler's triumph, for none of the other finalists could ride him. After two falls from the German horse, the Marquis di Medici for Italy retired, his compatriot Salvatore Oppes was third with Pagoro, and Captain de Fombelle of France second on Bucephale. Pagoro, a chestnut gelding, was champion horse, having gone clear with each rider. The first ever ladies' European title was won, at Spa, by Pat Smythe on Flanagan, an event she was later to win on four occasions.

In 1958 Douglas Bunn with a chestnut Irish horse called Sandy Point joined the British team. Only two years later he was to start the now world-famous All-England Jumping Course at Hickstead in Sussex.

Making its first appearance of the year at Aachen, the British team consisted of Pat Smythe with Flanagan and Mr Pollard, Ted Edgar with Jane Summers, Wilf White with

Two of the horses which won the 1958 Prince of Wales Cup for America: on this page Nautical, ridden by Hugh Wiley, and (over page) Ksar d'Esprit with Bill Steinkraus

Nizefela, and Ted Williams with Dumbell – who gave him a very bad fall in which he broke a bone in his neck, so that he was out of the Nations' Cup. After a jump-off, the cup was won by Spain with 7 faults, from the USA with 16 and West Germany with 28. Italy was fourth, on 35, followed by Holland ($51\frac{1}{2}$) while Britain brought up the rear with 52.

The European Championship was also held in Aachen, where it was very much dominated by the Germans with victory going to Fritz Thiedemann on Meteor, who defeated the holder, Hans Winkler with Halla, into third place. The championship was held under a somewhat different formula this time, on a points aggregate. Runner-up, with 98·3 points to the winner's 106, was Piero d'Inzeo on the great grey Irish horse, The Rock.

The ladies' European title, held at Palermo, was won for Italy by Giulia Serventi on Doly, who had been second for the title the previous year. Anna Clement of West Germany was second on Nico, and Holland was third, represented by Irene Jansen on Adelboom.

The season was notable for the appearance of a junior team from South Africa, of which the star was Gonda Butters, then fourteen years old. She had a great deal of success in England, riding against adults on her little chestnut Oorskiet. Although previous visitors from South Africa – notably David Stubbs, Bob Grayston and Mickey Louw – had been very successful, 1958 was the last year in which horses were able to travel freely between the two countries, due to the horse sickness ban.

At the Royal International Show at the White City, the Prince of Wales Cup went to the young team from the United States. The American horses consisted of Hugh Wiley's palomino, Nautical, a 16-hand horse with china-blue eyes, bred in New Mexico; the gigantic grey thoroughbred Ksar d'Esprit, nearly 18 hands high and a truly majestic animal; Night Owl and Sinjon. Hugh Wiley won the King George V Cup in 1958 for the first time, riding the grey Master William, a 17-hand thoroughbred, foaled in 1948. Not entirely dependable, he was a horse who, on his day, could be very good indeed. Wiley started jumping Shetland ponies when he was six, encouraged by a horse-minded grand-

43

Ksar d'Esprit with Bill Steinkraus

father, and first rode with the team in 1950. He also rode Hollandia and Ksar d'Esprit, a horse he bred himself.

Britain redressed the balance in Dublin two weeks later by winning the Aga Khan Trophy from the Americans with what can only be described as a scratch team: George Hobbs on Royal Lord, Jill Banks on Earlsrath Rambler, Marshall Charlesworth, a young farmer from Cheshire, on Smokey Bob, and Harvey Smith – another newcomer who was destined to become a household name – riding Farmer's Boy which he had bought under the hammer for £40.

This was Britain's sole Nations' Cup victory of the year. At Rotterdam, Peter Robeson with Ballymullan, Douglas Bunn with Sandy Point, Mary Barnes with Sudden and Wilf White with Nizefela got no higher than sixth out of six competing nations. The winners, with 21, were France; West Germany was runner-up on $24\frac{1}{4}$. Colonel Dan Corry returned to the Irish team and enabled them to beat the Americans. Britain's only consolation in Rotterdam was provided by Ann Townsend, only a year out of the junior team, who won the ladies' class.

The long winter months were enlivened by a new event called the Inter-Continental Championship of the Americas. Pat Smythe and Colonel C. H. 'Monkey' Blacker represented Britain. Most of the leading riders in Europe flew out to Viña del Mar, to be mounted from a pool of Chilean, Argentinian and Columbian horses. Two riders had the rare good fortune to draw their own horses – Dr Hugo Arrambide of the Argentine drew S'Il Vous Plait, and Captain Gaston Zuniga of Chile drew Pillan. They finished respectively third and fourth, being beaten by Europeans Pierre Jonquères d'Oriola and Colonel 'Monkey' Blacker, riding Argentine horses, Virrey and Stromboli. Among those to finish down the course were Hans Günter Winkler and his wife; Paco Goyoaga, Pedro Mayorga and Piero d'Inzeo.

The 1959 season was the precursor to the Rome Olympics and all the top nations were training hard. In April British riders assembled with their horses at Arundel Castle to train under Colonel Talbot-Ponsonby and, in May, set off on their first tour, to Lisbon and Madrid. The Americans, back in Europe again, were even quicker off the mark and took in Rome, where they beat the home side in the Nations'

Cup with a zero score to Italy's 8 faults.

In Lisbon, the Nations' Cup went to Spain, with $20\frac{1}{4}$ faults to Britain's 28, and Portugal third on 44. Individually there were many British triumphs, notably Ann Townsend, who was leading lady rider and won the Doubles and Trebles on her newly acquired Bandit IV, and Pat Smythe, who won the Grand Prix on Flanagan, from Marshall Charlesworth on Smokey Bob and Colonel Blacker on Workboy. A former 'chaser, Workboy was first ridden by Colonel Blacker in a school over hurdles as a four-year-old. Blacker was so thrilled by the way Workboy jumped that he vowed to own him one day, but the price at that time was £2,000, for this horse had obvious potential and was destined to become one of the best two-mile 'chasers in the country. For three seasons Workboy held sway, winning some £7,000 in stakes, then he strained a tendon and Colonel Blacker was able to buy him in 1955 for a mere £130. He came up as good as new after being fired and turned away, and started his new vocation in Germany. Lisbon, 1959, was Workboy's first international show – and his rider's second – and he won the Fault-and-Out.

In Madrid, Smokey Bob, Hollandia, Workboy and Flanagan won the Nations' Cup with 32 faults. Spain (39) were second, followed by West Germany (52), Portugal (78), France ($79\frac{1}{2}$) and Switzerland (106). Ann Townsend was leading rider once again, and put up an outstanding performance with Bandit to win the puissance after four barrages. In the last, they were the only pair to jump a spread of 6ft 6in by 7ft 2in, and the wall at 6ft 7in. The most impressive of all the British team horses was Hollandia, veteran of the US Olympic team in 1952 and acquired by Dawn Palethorpe on her marriage to Warren Wofford. This superb old horse won the second competition in Madrid with the fastest clear round, was second to Bandit in the puissance, won the Six Bars with the last fence at 5ft 11in and finally avenged his defeat by Bandit by winning the Grand Prix from him in a two-horse finish.

The next confrontation was in Paris, where Ann Townsend and Bandit continued their triumphant progress. She was leading lady rider for the third time off the reel, and put up the best British performance with two clear rounds in the Nations' Cup, where her team-mates were Dawn Wofford, Marshall Charlesworth and Douglas Bunn. In a real turn-up for the book, the Soviet Union had a flash-in-the-pan victory for only 4½ faults, to defeat West Germany (8¼), the United States (12), and Italy. Britain came fifth, followed by Spain, France, and Sweden.

At Aachen the Nations' Cup went to Italy, who had 7 faults to the Americans' 16, with no British team competing. In London, the American quartet won the Prince of Wales Cup for the second successive year, and Hugh Wiley, this time on Nautical, took the King George V Cup for the second year running. Nautical fairly swept the board during that week at the White City, winning also the *Horse & Hound* Cup and the *Daily Mail* Cup, and capturing both the points awards, the Saddle of Honour and the Loriners' Cup. Ann Townsend and Bandit were runners-up for both points championships, winners of the Distaff Stakes and equal first with Dawn Wofford on Hollandia in the Lonsdale Puissance. It was the first time this event had been won by a woman, let alone two; they each cleared the 6ft 6in wall that had caught out both Nautical and Alan Oliver's Red Admiral – the pair Piero d'Inzeo always considered he had to beat in order to win.

The Americans missed Dublin in order to compete in the Pan-American Games, in Chicago, where Bill Steinkraus on Riviera Wonder, Hugh Wiley on Nautical, Frank Chapot on the German-bred, ex-Thiedemann horse Diamant and George Marris on Night Owl won the team gold medals with 32 faults to 59 for Brazil; Chile, the Argentine and Venezuela followed on.

Meanwhile, in Dublin, Britain won the Aga Khan Trophy with 32 faults from Spain with 44 and Ireland with 51. At Le Zoute and Rotterdam, some new British riders came to the fore, among them David Barker, and David Broome, the future world champion, each making his first trip abroad.

In Rotterdam David Broome achieved his first international victories, taking the two-horse competition on Wildfire and Ballan Silver Knight, another event on Wildfire – and emerging as the leading rider. Wildfire, a somewhat remarkable leading national winner of the year, had been drafted from the King's Troop, RHA, for consistent insubordination, and was believed to be a confirmed stopper. Foaled in 1949, a 16-hand bay of un-

known breeding, Wildfire was a quality little horse, as compact and active as his successors, Sportsman and Ballywillwill. Fred Broome, David's father, bought him for £75 after seeing the horse stop six times over a 3ft fence, in September 1957. After a winter spent schooling and conditioning him, for Wildfire was not an easy horse to feed, he came out a reformed character in 1958, though he still swished his tail, squealed when he started his round and wore his ears laid neatly back along his neck. He won some major classes, and a year later was virtually unbeatable.

Franco, David Barker's first international horse, still going strong and winning international speed classes for Caroline Bradley, is a dark brown thoroughbred by Como. David bought him as a hunter, selling him on to a lady who returned him as he was bad in traffic. Riding Franco during the latter part of the hunting season, David discovered that he had a great 'pop' in him, and started to jump him in the ring. The horse went to his first show in May 1958, and was grade A by August, winning the international championship at Southport while still a novice. The following year he was selected for Olympic training.

Other promising young riders emerging in this pre-Olympic year included Lady Sarah Fitzalan-Howard. Riding the Little South African horse, Oorskiet, she was equal first for the individual Junior European Championship in London and selected to ride in Rotterdam, where she won two competitions. At the Horse of the Year Show, which moved that year from Harringay to its present home at Wembley, she won the Harringay Spurs, from no less a personage than Captain Piero d'Inzeo, for points gained throughout the week.

In December came the announcement of the final British Olympic candidates: Colonel 'Monkey' Blacker with Workboy, Pat Smythe with Flanagan and the Hon Mrs Edward Kidd's Grand Manan, Wilf White with Nizefela and Scorchin', David Broome with Wildfire, Ann Townsend with Bandit, David Barker with Franco, and Marshall Charlesworth with Smokey Bob.

The system of staging Olympic Trials was replaced in 1960 by Olympic Practices at various selected shows. The first was at Badminton, where Colonel Talbot-Ponsonby put up a really stiff course with a particularly

The unconventional style of Sunsalve, who won for David Broome both an Olympic bronze medal and a European Championship

testing treble. This revealed that one or two riders were approaching the time when they might be considered, in the Olympic context, to be 'over the hill'. Ted Edgar summed it up succinctly when he said: 'There hasn't been such a massacre since Mons!'

The possibles soon gave way to the probables, and the Olympic team candidates concluded their training, inestimably strengthened by a new horse for David Broome in the shape of Elizabeth Anderson's big, rangy chestnut, Sunsalve. A full brother to Colonel Harry Llewellyn's St David, he jumped in unconventional style, with his back as flat as a board, but though he sometimes was caught out in combinations he had an enormous jump and usually managed to get or keep himself out of trouble. David loves a quality horse and only days after they made one another's acquaintance they won the King George V Gold Cup. It became clear that David Broome and Sunsalve had even stronger claim than David Broome and Wildfire for inclusion in Britain's Olympic team. Those who finally arrived in Rome for the Olympic Games in early September were Broome with Sunsalve, Pat Smythe with Flanagan and Scorchin', Dawn Wofford with Hollandia and David Barker with Franco.

6 The Years to Tokio 1960~1964

West Germany, with two consecutive Olympic victories behind them, inevitably started as favourites in the Prix des Nations – especially as Hans Gunter Winkler with Halla and Fritz Thiedemann with Meteor were still in the first flight, and their third man, Alwin Schockemöhle, riding Ferdl, had been selected as the most promising of a fairly formidable rearguard force of younger riders.

For the first time since Antwerp in 1920, there were to be two separate Olympic show jumping occasions – the individual taking place in the famous Piazza di Siena, home of the Italian Concours Hippique Internationale Officiale (CHIO), while the team event would be staged in the Olympic Stadium immediately before the closing ceremony of the Games.

In the individual contest over a trappy course, with a long double after a big upright and a toll-taking treble of wall-triple-to-parallels, Raimondo d'Inzeo received an ecstatic ovation when, on his chestnut thoroughbred Posillipo, he achieved what was to remain the first and last clear round of the day. At the end of the first round, after Winkler with Halla and Thiedemann with Meteor had knocked up 17 and $13\frac{1}{2}$ faults respectively, second place was held by the Argentine Dasso on Final with 4 faults, while third place, on 8, was disputed by Piero d'Inzeo on The Rock, then one of the best puissance horses in the world, and Colonel Max Fresson on Grand Veneur. Broome and Sunsalve had four fences down for 16 faults.

The first round had started at 7 am, but throughout the second the sun was blazing down. Raimondo d'Inzeo and Posillipo had three down to total 12, Piero on The Rock duplicated their first-round score of 8, but Colonel Fresson dropped back in the reckoning with a cricket score of $29\frac{1}{4}$. Then, with the d'Inzeo brothers lying first and second – Dasso and Final having gone to pieces for 24 – David Broome put up the best performance of the second round to finish third on Sunsalve to give Britain the individual bronze medal.

Pat Smythe on Flanagan and Dawn Wofford on Hollandia finished the individual disputing eleventh and twentieth places respectively, and on this form David Barker and Franco were given preference over Hollandia for the team event – a decision which was to have disastrous repercussions. The psychological effect on the participants of an Olympic

The d'Inzeo brothers, who have consistently won medals and titles for Italy for over twenty years: seen here, Raimondo on the Italian-bred Posillipo and Piero on the Irish horse, The Rock, over page

Prix des Nations has to be experienced to be believed. When a rider first emerges into the arena, entirely alone before 10,000 spectators, it is easy to be overawed by the occasion. And when a competitor has not had the advantage of a preliminary canter in the individual Grand Prix – as was the case with David Barker – the impact of being flung in at the deep end to sink or swim is overpowering.

Eighteen teams were involved in the Prix des Nations, which started nearly an hour late. The first competitor, a Turk, was carried from the ring on a stretcher. David Barker was No 2 in the draw. Franco, sensing his rider's tension, started off on his round like a wooden horse. After jumping the first two elements of the treble, No 5, he stopped at the third, repeating the performance at his second attempt. At his third try he jumped it, and continued on his way without further incident until the very last of the fourteen fences, where he stopped again for elimination. An eliminated rider was given the worst score in the round, plus an extra 20 faults, so Britain's chances were already lost. The one bright spot was to be the showing of David Broome

and Sunsalve who jumped what appeared to be a clear round. A zero score was shown on the board when Sunsalve left the ring, but later this was altered to a 4, the judges insisting that he had dropped a foot in the water.

At the end of the first round, West Germany led with $25\frac{3}{4}$ faults, both Ferdl and Meteor incurring faults at the water, No 7, which took a heavy toll throughout. It also caught Bill Steinkraus on the US puissance specialist, Ksar d'Esprit, who had felled both parts of the double. But the American team remained very much in the picture, in second place with 29 faults. Italy was third on $52\frac{1}{2}$ after a long gap, for though Posillipo was round in 4, The Rock had 24 faults, and Oppes with The Scholar was $\frac{1}{2}$ fault behind him.

In the second round the United States dropped back a little, while the Germans consolidated their position. Meteor rallied his forces for 8, Ferdl did the same for $8\frac{3}{4}$, and the great Halla was clear but for a tap at the last fence. Thus West Germany won her third consecutive Olympic Prix des Nations with only $46\frac{1}{2}$ faults to the 66 of the United States silver medallists. Italy with $80\frac{1}{2}$ won the bronze medals largely due to Posillipo, who with only one mistake in each round achieved the best individual performance. The United Arab Republic was fourth ($135\frac{1}{2}$); the only other teams to finish were France ($168\frac{3}{4}$) and Rumania ($174\frac{1}{2}$). Twelve nations were eliminated, nine of them in the first round.

Shortly after the Olympic Games, the World Championship was held in Venice, where David Broome and Sunsalve went through to the final, accompanied by Bill Steinkraus on Ksar d'Esprit, Colonel Carlos Delia of the Argentine on Huipil, and Raimondo d'Inzeo on the eight-year-old Irish bay, Gowran Girl. This latter was not an easy mare to ride; Delia knocked up 12 faults on her, and Broome and Steinkraus each had four down. Raimondo d'Inzeo's successful defence of the title he had won in Aachen four years earlier cost him only 8 faults.

In Britain the most significant happening in 1960 was the opening of Douglas Bunn's All England Jumping Course at Hickstead, Sussex, now the most famous permanent show jumping centre in the world. Bunn had long been conscious that British horses and riders suffered considerably from the fact that there was no permanent course of true international fences in England. When teams went abroad and faced natural obstacles, such as banks, tables, road fences and stone walls, they were at a great disadvantage, their horses only finding their form over these strange hazards when it was time to go home.

With great enterprise and foresight and not a little courage, Bunn bought a lovely old house with some land and set about building a first-class international arena – bigger than any on the Continent – with natural obstacles. The feature event at Hickstead was to be the British Jumping Derby over a long and difficult course of big fences, dominated by an enormous bank which would only be negotiated once a year. When Hickstead's gates first opened in May 1960, the show jumping fraternity, impelled by curiosity, turned up on their feet, but there were very few entries. The facilities were primitive, and criticism was rife on all sides. With a hard core of supporters to encourage him, however, Bunn was wise enough to play a waiting game, and the success of his venture was assured in 1961, when W. D. & H. O. Wills undertook the sponsorship of the All England Jumping Course.

Over the years, the amenities at Hickstead have increased and improved. Numerous continental championships and world titles have been fought out there; only one of the four meetings held each season is not a fully-fledged international show. The American team has made Hickstead its base on many occasions, and Raimondo d'Inzeo told me that in his opinion it is the finest show jumping centre he has ever seen.

The British Jumping Derby was an instant success. Now one of the most richly endowed competitions in the world, with total stakes of £6,000 and a first prize of £2,000, it has become to show jumping what the Grand National is to National Hunt racing. The 10ft 6in Derby Bank has been the object of a good deal of discussion with its near-sheer descent. Alison Dawes, the first rider ever to come down it, was only seventeen at the time. She has since, with The Maverick, become one of the four dual winners, the others being Seamus Hayes of Ireland with Goodbye, who won the inaugural competition in 1961, Nelson Pessoa of Brazil with Gran Geste, and Harvey Smith with Mattie Brown, the winner for two successive years.

Douglas Bunn, responsible for the building of the All England Course at his home at Hickstead, riding Beethoven

At Aachen in 1961 David Broome and Sunsalve won the Men's European Championship, their nearest rival being Piero d'Inzeo with the grey Irish horse, Pioneer. Five fought out the final: Captain Callado of Portugal on Konak, Winkler on the grey Hanoverian Romanus, and Graziano Mancinelli for Italy on the grey Irish mare, Rockette. With a brilliant recovery in the treble, Sunsalve was clear to win in 36·7 secs; d'Inzeo was already assured of second place overall and opted out of the final round, and Winkler finished third. It was a notable and hard-won victory for David. Fred Broome told me later that Sunsalve was not his usual self for weeks afterwards – indeed, he did not find his true form again that season, and during the winter he died of a heart attack.

Pat Smythe, in Deauville, rode Flanagan to regain the ladies' European title, while a five-year series of British triumphs in the Junior European Championship was ended at Hickstead by West Germany, followed home by Holland, with the host side third.

Piero d'Inzeo and The Rock won the first of two successive victories in the King George V Gold Cup, while the Queen Elizabeth Cup

Seamus Hayes on Goodbye, winners of the first British Jumping Derby in 1961

went to Lady Sarah Fitzalan-Howard on Oorskiet. The Rock, who had won the Italian Grand Prix in 1958, his second international season, also took the Grand Prix at Aachen. The Rome Grand Prix went to Ireland's Captain Billy Ringrose on the outstanding chestnut Loch an Easpaig, who began to put the Irish Army back on the map again but dropped dead of a heart attack in the ring at Ostend during the 1967 Nations' Cup.

The Irish had previously won the Nations' Cup in Nice, the West Germans winning in Aachen, Dublin and Geneva – in each case from Italy, the winners in London – and Ostend. Britain's sole victory was gained at Rotterdam, where Valerie Clark (now Mrs David Barker) won the Grand Prix on her bay Irish mare, Atlanta, in her first international show abroad. In New York, the Argentine trounced the home side for the Nations' Cup, but the United States regained their ascendancy in Toronto.

In 1962, the Men's European Championship was held in London. Without Sunsalve, David Broome was considered not to have a suitable horse and was not chosen to defend

The most successful of the post-war Irish riders, Capt Billy Ringrose on Loch an Easpaig, who died in the ring during the 1967 Nations' Cup

the title he had won in Aachen. The pair selected were Peter Robeson with Firecrest, a chestnut who had previously won the Scottish Points Championship for three years in succession, and David Barker on Mister Softee, one of the 'greats' whose record in this championship still stands unchallenged. The final was contested over two rounds of a fourteen-fence, Nations' Cup-type course, and in the first innings the only clear rounds were recorded by Barker with Mister Softee and Piero d'Inzeo with The Rock. In the second round The Rock made two mistakes, but Softee's only fault came at the final double of parallels, and he thus gained the title. The Rock and Hans Gunter Winkler's Romanus finished disputing second place, and Peter Robeson with Firecrest finished equal fourth with Raimondo d'Inzeo on Posillipo.

In 1962 the United States team engaged on a European tour, when Bill Steinkraus, Frank Chapot and Hugh Wiley were accompanied by two extremely accomplished lady riders in Kathy Kusner, later to become the first American girl to get a jockey's licence, and Mary Mairs (now Mrs Frank Chapot). They started well by winning the Nations' Cup at Aachen, but the Germans had their revenge in London where the United States tied for second place with Italy. In Dublin, the Italians won from the Americans, with Britain third, so the honours were well spread and no team had everything its own way. The British junior team, which travelled to Berlin to win back the European title, was notable for the first international appearance of Marion Coakes with her phenomenal pony Stroller.

In 1963 the Men's European Championship, held in the Piazza di Siena in Rome, was won for the home side by Graziano Mancinelli with Rockette. Alwin Schockemohle was runner-up with Freiherr. Harvey Smith finished third on the former Canadian horse, O'Malley. Having joined Harvey Smith's string in July 1962, O'Malley won the John Player Trophy, the Grand Prix, at the Royal International. A difficult horse, he was nevertheless the top money-winner in Britain in 1963 and 1964.

A young British team was now fusing together. One of its most remarkable members was Anneli Drummond-Hay with the majestic-looking brown horse, Merely-a-Monarch, by

Tommy Wade on Dundrum, a horse who proved lack of size was no handicap by winning many trophies in the early 1960s

Anneli Drummond-Hay on Merely-a-Monarch: this famous partnership was equally successful in eventing and show jumping

the premium stallion Happy Monarch, on whom she had already won the Three-Day Events at Burghley and Badminton. In 1962, she switched to show jumping from combined training in order to ride in the Olympic Games – women at that time being debarred from competing in the Olympic Three-Day Event. Making a remarkable changeover, Merely-a-Monarch won the Imperial Cup at the Royal International Horse Show. In Rome the following year he jumped two clear rounds which helped to win the Nations' Cup, and he enabled Anneli to finish third in the European Ladies' Championship, then held at Hickstead.

Britain had a successful record in European Nations' Cups in 1963, winning in Rome, London, Ostend and Rotterdam, and registering its first victory in the Prince of Wales Cup since 1957. Ireland won the Aga Khan Trophy in Dublin, for the first time since 1949, a contributory factor being the two clear rounds jumped by the Hon Diana Conolly-Carew riding Barrymore, a grey gelding. In Lisbon he jumped 6ft 6in to win the puissance, and was runner-up for the Queen Elizabeth Cup and for the 1965 British Jumping Derby at

Hickstead, where his only error was to bank the privet oxer – not an unnatural mistake for an Irish horse.

Ireland's really great individual partnership at this time was that of Tommy Wade and Dundrum, a bay gelding only 15 hands $1\frac{1}{2}$in high, named after the town not far from Dublin where he started life pulling a milk float. First upgraded at the Irish country shows in 1957, Dundrum later won two international and nine national championships in Dublin, where he became a national hero, and three at the Royal Ulster show in Belfast. His triumphs in London were initiated at the Horse of the Year Show in 1961, where he won the Victor Ludorum. A year later he won the White Horse Puissance and the Guinness Time Championship at Wembley, the Vaux Gold Tankard at the Royal Highland Show at Edinburgh and the Grand Prix in Ostend and Brussels. At Ostend he won every competition in which he was started. In 1963 he won the King George V Cup at the Royal International and the White Horse Puissance for the second year running, and was well on the way to winning the Wills British Jumping Derby at Hickstead when he burst a blood vessel during the barrage and had to be withdrawn.

Piero d'Inzeo had some stormy passages with the Italian federation, which caused him to be grounded in 1963. His brother Raimondo won the Aachen Grand Prix on Posillipo; the runner-up, in her first season after riding with the French Junior team, was Janou Lefebvre (now Mme Tissot) with Kenavo. She made the transition from junior to senior classes with a notable panache, winning the Grand Prix at Dinard and the French Jumping Derby at La Baule.

The United States team, warming up for the Tokyo Olympics, won both the team and individual gold medals at the Pan-American Games in São Paulo. Mary Mairs was the individual winner, riding the chestnut mare Tomboy, who could jump big fences and was also possessed of a fair turn of speed. A beautiful stylist, Mary Mairs beat Carlos Delia of the Argentine on Popin for the individual gold medal, and was a member of the team – with Bill Steinkraus on Sinjon, Kathy Kusner on Unusual, and Frank Chapot on San Lucas – which won with $44\frac{1}{4}$ faults from the Argentine ($52\frac{1}{2}$) and Chile (69).

In Washington not long afterwards Mary Mairs and Tomboy won the international championship, while in New York the Grand Prix went to a Canadian girl, Gail Ross, on her chestnut seven-year-old Thunderbird. After taking the international championship at the Royal Winter Fair in Toronto, she became a popular competitor on the English show jumping circuit. Canadian jumping also received a fillip when Tommy Gayford set up the High Jump record of 7ft 1in in New York on Blue Beau, a horse who had jumped on the Canadian team for ten seasons.

The 1964 Olympic Games did not take place until October and for some nations – including Britain – the interval proved to be too long. Horses dropped out like the ten little nigger boys and, when the time came, the selectors were hard pushed to send a team to Tokyo at all. It had been easy enough to produce a short list of twelve the previous winter, but only one of them, Peter Robeson's Firecrest, was ultimately selected. After the first trial of the year on bone-hard going, Mister Softee, then Britain's brightest hope, was out for the rest of the season and the first to drop from the list. Oddly enough, though he possessed what were arguably the worst hind legs in the business, they never let him down, and when he was unsound it was always in front.

The best performance in the second trial was that of Andrew Fielder and his enormous, back-kicking Vibart, a 17·2hh bay gelding by the thoroughbred Hyross, a winner over hurdles, out of a Clydesdale mare. Andrew first rode him when he was only fifteen and Vibart was the nearest thing to a rogue, but in 1963 he was in the winning British team for the Junior European Championship in Rotterdam. At Wembley he won the most controversial competition ever staged for the Leading Show Jumper title; for which Colonel Talbot-Ponsonby built a very difficult course, fairly bristling with related fences. Vibart was the only one to take it in his enormous stride, to win with the only clear round. His rider also won the Wembley Spurs for the points aggregate gained throughout the week on one horse. Vibart's ticket to Tokyo seemed assured after the trials, but it was discovered then that Andrew Fielder, still only seventeen, was too young to be eligible for an Olympic Games.

He was, however, a member of the British team which travelled to Aachen. There Harvey Smith was the only British winner,

Bill Steinkraus and Sinjon, winners of the 1962
King George v Gold Cup

riding his grey speed horse, The Sea Hawk, a former champion hack in South Africa. In the Nations' Cup, Italy came first, followed by West Germany, Spain, France and Britain. The leading rider was Nelson Pessoa of Brazil, who on his grey Gran Geste won the Grand Prix d'Europe – a substitute event for the European Championship, never held in an Olympic year – and the Aachen Grand Prix.

The Americans arrived in Europe in time to jump at the Royal International, where Bill Steinkraus won his second King George V Cup on the bay Sinjon, who had been the leading horse on the 1962 European tour. Sadly he failed to pull out quite sound in Tokyo and grounded his rider for the Olympic Prix des Nations.

Italy, having won the Nations' Cup in Rome as well as Aachen, started favourites for the Prince of Wales Cup in London, but Britain achieved a zero score after double clear rounds by Peter Robeson with Firecrest, Elizabeth Broome on Jacopo (owned by her future husband, Ted Edgar) and David Boston Barker on North Riding. Italy, with the d'Inzeos and Mancinelli, was runner-up and the United States third. In Dublin, where Kathy Kusner and Untouchable initiated a two-year hold on the Grand Prix, the United States team won the Aga Khan Trophy from Britain, and in Rotterdam the West Germans beat them both.

Thus the field was fairly open for the Olympic Games. Britain was still havering about her team. At the White City, Merely-a-Monarch was tried out by David Broome, but what could have been a useful partnership was not allowed to proceed beyond the experimental stage, as clearly all was not well with this brilliant horse. Eventually David was partnered by Ted Edgar's Jacopo, whose saddle his sister had been keeping warm to win the National Championship and the Lonsdale Puissance at the White City. Peter Robeson and Firecrest were a certainty, but all was not well with O'Malley, and Harvey Smith was overlooked by the selectors. The third rider chosen was David Boston Barker with North Riding. His younger brother William, fresh from his triumph in the Young Riders' Championship of Great Britain at Hickstead, was selected as reserve on his half-Cleveland bay mare, North Flight.

In Tokyo there was no individual show

Paul Robeson on Firecrest, bronze medallists at the Tokyo Olympics jumping competition. Individual awards, as at Wembley in 1948, were dependent upon the placings in the team event. The going was tricky after a considerable amount of rain, and the fourteen fences looked less than inviting, in particular the treble with big spreads both in and out, and the final parallels at the maximum 4ft 11in with a wall between them and a spread of 5ft 9in.

There were fourteen teams in the field, Australia being represented for the first time ever, and four individuals. The best score in the first innings was 8 faults. Sharing the individual lead were Peter Robeson with Firecrest, John Fahey of Australia with a wiry little brown waler called Bonvale, and Portugal's Duarte Silva on Jeune France. D'Oriola had not only faulted at the water, No 13, and the last fence, but also incurred a time fault. Mary Mairs and Tomboy gave a most uncharacteristic performance for $44\frac{1}{2}$ faults, which put paid to America's chances. David Broome got Jacopo round in 16, but Barker and North Riding knocked up $28\frac{1}{4}$. At the halfway stage West Germany was in the lead with $39\frac{3}{4}$ faults, then Italy (44), France (45), Britain ($52\frac{1}{4}$) and Australia ($53\frac{1}{2}$).

In the second round both Bonvale and Firecrest stayed level on 8, while Jeune France dropped behind with 12. Hermann Schridde on Dozent went clear for West Germany, with $1\frac{1}{4}$ time faults to add, which gave them the individual silver medal, and their team another gold. The individual gold went to Pierre d'Oriola, who went clear, within the time with ·5 secs to spare, on Lutteur B, an amazing first-season international horse, who had earlier won the French Jumping Derby and the Spanish Grand Prix. Robeson and Fahey jumped off for the individual bronze, Firecrest going clear and faster than Bonvale, who had two down. The final team result was West Germany victorious with $68\frac{1}{2}$ faults, France (d'Oriola on Lutteur B, Guy Lefrant on M. de Littry and Janou Lefebvre on Kenavo) second on $77\frac{3}{4}$ faults, and Italy (Piero d'Inzeo on Sunbeam, Raimondo on Posillipo and Mancinelli on Rockette) third on $88\frac{1}{2}$. Britain finished fourth, followed by the Argentine and the United States.

7 On to Mexico 1965~1968

The beginning of another Olympic cycle, 1965 was notable for the equine influenza epidemic. This kept the British team away from Nice and Rome where Italy's victories gave them a head start in the newly instituted world team championship for the President's Cup, initiated by HRH the Duke of Edinburgh, who had succeeded Prince Bernhard of The Netherlands as President of the Fédération Equestre Internationale.

In view of the travelling problems encountered by several nations, it was decided that the cup should be awarded on a points basis and that only the best six performances of each country should be valid for qualification. Although Italy also won at Aachen and London, Britain gained the trophy as a result of her victories at Madrid, Dublin, Copenhagen, Rotterdam, Ostend and Olsztyn in Poland. In its first venture behind the Iron Curtain – where the standard is much below that in the West – the British team were given a warm welcome, and this pioneering trip was subsequently repeated.

In the King George V Cup, Douglas Bunn and Beethoven jumped off before ceding victory to Hans Günter Winkler on Fortun, while the Queen Elizabeth Cup went to Marion Coakes and Stroller, who won by a whisker (one-tenth of a second) from Alison Westwood with The Maverick, leading combination in Aachen, London, Rotterdam, Enschede and Geneva. Only weeks later, at Hickstead, Marion (aged seventeen) and Stroller (only $14 \cdot 1\frac{1}{2}$hh) – the youngest rider and smallest horse in the field – won the first ever Women's World Championship. Stroller survived three days over big fences and defeated the favourite, Kathy Kusner of the US on the thoroughbred chestnut gelding Untouchable.

Stroller, a brown Irish pony, foaled in 1953, was first ridden by Marion in 1960 and when, in 1964, she had to graduate from the junior classes, she persuaded her father to allow the pony to go on into adult competitions with her to see if he could cope with the bigger fences and longer distances. Not only did he cope, but in his first season in open classes he was runner-up to Seamus Hayes of Ireland on Goodbye in the British Jumping Derby at Hickstead. This was Stroller's happiest hunting ground, where he won the Wills Gold Medal, for points gained in the major international classes during the season, on no

Marion Coakes and Stroller, World Champions
in 1965 despite being the youngest rider and
smallest horse in the field

fewer than five occasions on the trot – a record unlikely to be challenged. When he retired officially from the ring in 1973, a special ceremony to mark the occasion was staged at Hickstead before the start of the British Jumping Derby.

The Men's European Championship, held in Aachen, was won by Hermann Schridde on his Olympic horse, Dozent, after both Pierre d'Oriola and Nelson Pessoa were eliminated for taking the wrong course. Runner-up, for Spain, was Alfonso Queipo de Llano on Infernal, who had won the Rome Grand Prix the previous year. Third place went to the home side's Alwin Schokemöhle with Exact, who in Cologne had set the German high jump record, clearing 7ft 4in.

In North America, the United States team swept the board on the fall circuit, winning the Nations' Cups in Harrisburg, New York and Toronto. Bill Steinkraus had a great new horse in Snowbound, a brown thoroughbred gelding, who started his working life as a race-horse on the West Coast. He made his first trip to Europe as a member of the US team in 1964, when he was six. A year later he won the Grand Prix in New York and gained Bill

an individual gold medal in the 1968 Olympics. Frank Chapot won the North American Championship in Toronto on San Lucas, the biggest horse on the US team and the one to hold the longest record, having jumped with the team from 1961 until he was retired, with Snowbound, in the winter of 1973. A chestnut gelding, 17·3hh, San Lucas also started life as a racehorse. His first big success in the show ring was when he won the individual championship in New York in 1961. Thereafter he was to prove the mainstay of the team, particularly in Nations' Cups, Grand Prix and puissance competitions.

The 1966 season was also curtailed, more severely this time, by an outbreak of swamp fever in France. The British team had competed in Paris in March, winning the Nations' Cup, thanks to two brilliant clear rounds by Ted Williams on Carnaval, an Argentine-bred chestnut owned by Frank Smith. The horse had only just recovered from running a nail into his foot in the collecting ring; frequent poulticing, day and night, got him right in time, and Ted was chaired by his team-mates after his well-earned victory. He became even more of a hero to the French

Frank Chapot of the US team and the huge San Lucas, whose career spanned a decade

after an official in charge of the public address system, having asked a British rider how old Ted Williams was, received the jovial, if inaccurate, reply: 'Seventy-five!' Thereafter Ted received a good deal of unwelcome publicity as the oldest rider in the show.

The Americans made a whistle-stop tour of the major continental shows, missing out Dublin and London because of the swamp-fever restrictions. They won the Nations' Cup in Lucerne and were second to Italy in Aachen, where a new team member, Neal Shapiro, scored his first international win by taking the Grand Prix on a little-known horse called Jacks or Better.

For Pierre d'Oriola the long journey from the Pyrenees to Buenos Aires was made worthwhile when he won the Men's World Championship, held for the first time outside Europe. A young and inexperienced mare, Pomone, half-sister to his Olympic-winning Lutteur B, took him through to the final which he won with 16 faults, followed by Alvarez de Bohorques of Spain on Quizas (19). Nelson Pessoa who, on Huipil, came fifth with $35\frac{1}{4}$ faults, later won the European Championship on Gran Geste in Lucerne from Frank Chapot on San Lucas.

The Women's European Championship, held in Gijon, went to France, represented by Janou Lefebvre on Kenavo, with 3 points, from Switzerland's Monika Bachmann (now Mrs Paul Weier) on Sandro, with 9. In third place, with $10\frac{1}{2}$, was Lalla Novo from Italy with the Irish horse Oxo Bob. For the first time since 1958 there were no British girls in the field, and this was the first non-British victory since that date.

At the 1965 Horse of the Year Show, David Broome had made his first international appearance on Mister Softee, who had won the Men's European title with David Barker in 1962. This was the beginning of a long and triumphant partnership and gave Broome his best horse since Sunsalve. In 1966 the pair were virtually unbeatable in all the big competitions in England. They won the King George V Cup; jumped the only clear round to win the British Jumping Derby at Hickstead; won the Olympic Trial at British Timken, and finally took the Ronson Victor Ludorum at the Horse of the Year Show.

The President's Cup for 1966 went to the United States, who won the Nations' Cups at Lucerne, New York and Harrisburg. At the

Royal Winter Fair in Toronto, however, they suffered a surprise defeat at the hands of the Canadians, whose success story continued at the Pan-American Games, when twenty-one-year-old Jimmy Day, the baby of the team, won the individual gold medal with the seven-year-old Canadian Club, after a jump-off with Nelson Pessoa on Gran Geste. Each had achieved double clear rounds, but the Canadian gained the verdict on time, being faster by just over a second. The Canadian team came third, after Brazil and the United States.

In 1967, the pre-Olympic year, Britain regained the President's Cup with six wins – at Nice, Olsztyn, Aachen, Leipzig, London and Rotterdam – in eight starts for the Nations' Cups of Europe. A very young team, with Caroline Bradley making her first international appearance, swung the result with their trip to Poland and East Germany.

As in Paris the previous year, it was Ted Williams who was instrumental in the British victory in Aachen, with a decisive clear round on Carnaval. The rest of the team consisted of Althea Roger Smith (now Mrs Josh Gifford)

on Havana Royal, who achieved two clears, John Baillie from Scotland with Dominic, and Andrew Fielder with Vibart. Germany's chances went when Schockemöhle's Donald Rex, a newcomer to the international scene, fell at the water. Italy finished as runners-up by $\frac{1}{2}$ fault in a very tight finish, with the United States third.

Fielder and Vibart were the first British pair ever to win the Aachen Grand Prix and also the Hamburg Jumping Derby a week later. At Aachen Mancinelli's best horse, Turvey, collapsed and died of heart failure, and at Hamburg Winkler fell and broke an arm in several places, each incident emphasising the role played by luck in show jumping competitions.

The Men's European Championship, held in Rotterdam, fell to the attack of David Broome and Mister Softee, with Harvey Smith as runner-up on his three-quarter-bred bay, Harvester V, and Alwin Schockemöhle third on Donald Rex. Broome's victory enabled the next championship, in 1969, to be held at Hickstead, where both horse and rider won their third successive title.

One of Britain's greatest partnerships – David Broome and Mr Softee, winners of an Olympic bronze medal and two European titles

The Women's Championship, held in Fontainebleau, was fought out without the world title holder, Marion Coakes with Stroller. The British selectors decided that it would be *infra dig* for the reigning world champion to compete, and possibly be defeated, for an inferior award. This line of reasoning seemed somewhat obscure at the time, although the same policy was followed by Janou Lefebvre of France, who after her victory on Rocket in Copenhagen in 1970 steadfastly declined to take a tilt at the European title. Britain was represented at Fontainebleau by Anneli Drummond-Hay on Merely-a-Monarch and by Alison Westwood with The Maverick, but neither was able to withstand the challenge of Kathy Kusner on Untouchable for the United States. Lalla Novo was second for Italy on Prédestiné and Monika Bachmann third for Switzerland on Erbach.

The Prince of Wales Cup was won by Britain from Italy, with Althea Roger Smith and Havana Royal achieving the only double clear round for the best individual performance. David Broome and Mister Softee failed to defend the cup successfully against Peter Robeson, who on Firecrest was able to realise one of his dearest ambitions. Harvey Smith was third on O'Malley, while Alan Oliver, staging a great comeback, finished fourth on Sweep. The King George V Cup, which Seamus Hayes had been trying to win for many years, finally eluded him when, having jumped clear on Goodbye, he forgot to jump the last fence.

At Hickstead, Marion Coakes and Stroller jumped the only clear round of the day to win the British Jumping Derby and, on Harvester, Harvey Smith was the leading money-winner for the fourth time in five years. In Dublin, where Ireland beat Britain for the Aga Khan Trophy, David Broome and Mister Softee won the first of two successive victories in the Irish Grand Prix, which in 1968 carried total stakes of £5,000 with £1,650 to the winner – the Royal Dublin Society having finally allowed competitions at Ball's Bridge to be sponsored by commercial enterprises.

After a lapse of ten years a British team was sent on the North American fall circuit. The Americans won the Nations' Cups in both New York and Toronto, but Harvey Smith and O'Malley carried off the Grand Prix in New York.

The Olympic Games in Mexico City which dominated everyone's hopes and ambitions in 1968 were preceded by some rare warming-up skirmishes both in Europe and the United States. The American team regained the President's Cup from Britain with wins in London, Dublin, Ostend and Rotterdam – the only team events they contested in Europe – while, after the Games, they won in New York and Toronto. Italy was an early winner in Europe, scoring at Nice and in Rome, where Anneli Drummond-Hay and the former Warwickshire hunter, Xanthos, won the women's European title from Italy's Giulia Serventi on Gay Monarch, with third place shared by Marion Coakes with Stroller and Janou Lefebvre on Rocket. The Rome Grand Prix went to Piero d'Inzeo and his Olympic horse, the hard-pulling and excitable German-bred Fidux, by a mere tenth of a second from Anneli Drummond-Hay on Merely-a-Monarch and Peter Robeson on Firecrest.

Italy scored again in the Nations' Cup at Aachen, narrowly defeating the German team, but it was in London that the real Olympic dress rehearsal took place. Wembley Stadium, where the Royal International was held this year, was not an ideal setting, with its vast empty stands and consequent lack of atmosphere, but there was a star cast of horses and riders from all the top nations. The West Germans did best individually, filling the first three places in the puissance, which was divided between Hans Güntcr Winkler on Enigk and Hartwig Steenken on Porta Westfalica. Enigk, an 'improved' Hanoverian by a thoroughbred sire, who had won the Aachen Grand Prix earlier in the month, took the King George V Gold Cup.

Neither the West Germans nor the Italians were going well in the Prince of Wales Cup, which developed into a duel between the American and British riders. In the first round they were on level pegging until Bill Steinkraus came in to jump the first clear on Snowbound, to put the United States ahead with 8 faults to Britain's 12. In the second round, Mary Chapot and White Lightning, on whom she had won the Queen Elizabeth Cup two days before, gave the United States another clear round. Although David Broome and Mister Softee replied in kind, Bill Steinkraus and Snowbound pulled off a double clear to give victory to the American team, with a grand total of 12 faults to Britain's 28, with Germany

Kathy Kusner of the USA who proved unbeatable in the European Championship of 1967

third on 36, Italy next on 51 and Ireland last with 55½. Snowbound set the seal on his week by winning the Daily Mail Cup, and in Dublin two weeks later jumped two clear rounds in the Aga Khan Trophy to lead his team to another victory over the British side. But then this remarkable horse went lame – the tendon which was to cause trouble throughout his career having caught up with him – and he had to miss Ostend and Rotterdam.

At Hickstead Alison Westwood and The Maverick jumped the only clear round to win the British Jumping Derby, and on this form were selected to travel to Mexico City as reserves for the British team, which consisted of Marion Coakes with Stroller, David Broome with Mister Softee and Harvey Smith with O'Malley and Madison Time. The individual competition, attracting forty-two starters, took place not in the Olympic stadium but in the Campo Marte, in a setting described by David Broome as very like that of an English country show. The contest was run under a new formula, with the first round jumped over a course of fourteen Nations' Cup-type fences. Then the best third – a hard core of eighteen horses and riders – tackled six puissance-type fences: a 5ft 11in wall at No 3; a parallel 5ft 7in by 7ft at No 5, and finally a big double, with a straight fence going in and an oxer coming out.

The first round produced only two clears – the first by Marion Coakes and Stroller, bouncing round as though they jumped Olympic courses every day of the week and tossing all the big fences behind them, and the second by Bill Steinkraus with Snowbound, more precise and less abandoned. Sharing second place with one mistake were David Broome and Mister Softee for Britain, Piero d'Inzeo on Fidux for Italy, Jimmy Day on Canadian Club for Canada, Kevin Baker on Chichester for Australia and Frank Chapot on San Lucas for the United States.

In the second round, Stroller just tapped a back pole of the huge parallel poles, and hit the oxer coming out of the final double, for 8 faults. Snowbound then put up a memorable performance, making his only error at the parallels for 4 faults. The gallant American horse was hopping lame when he finished the course and Bill Steinkraus had to ride in on a borrowed mount to receive his gold medal. With Stroller taking the silver, the winner of

Bill Steinkraus on Snowbound with Billy Haggard, owner of Main Spring. Snowbound was Steinkraus's gold medallist, taking the individual medal in Mexico City

the bronze medal had still to be decided. Four jumped off against the clock and all went clear: Chapot and San Lucas in 36·8 secs, Winkler and Enigk in 37·5, Jim Elder and The Immigrant in 39·2 and finally Broome and Mister Softee in the best time of 35·3.

The course for the fifteen competing teams was somewhat bigger than that set for the individual, but the main difficulty lay in the siting of the fences. The treble, at No 7, preceded by a big triple bar only five strides away, consisted of a wall at 5ft, and two big parallels, each at 4ft 11in and with spreads of 5ft 7in and 5ft 11in respectively. The water, No 11, was 16ft 3in wide followed, six strides later, by a double of true parallels, each 4ft 9in, with spreads of 5ft 7in and 5ft 9in. The time allowed was very tight.

Only four horses survived the first round with two fences down: San Lucas, Enigk, The Immigrant and Mister Softee – who was the only one not to incur time faults. Harvey Smith and Madison Time were round with 18¼ faults, and Stroller, who was the first to clear the big spread of water but had a stop at the double, had 21¾. At the halfway mark

The winning Canadian team in the 1968
Olympics: from left to right, Moffat Dunlap,
Tommy Gayford, Jimmy Day and Jim Elder

Britain led with 48 faults, closely followed by Canada with $49\frac{1}{2}$; France was third on $56\frac{1}{2}$, then came West Germany ($58\frac{1}{4}$), the USA (63) and Italy (64).

Disaster for Britain came in the second innings, when little Stroller stopped at the second part of the treble. At his second attempt he stopped again, this time hurling his rider into the poles. Half-dazed, Marion remounted and went again, but though this time Stroller was safely through the treble the time limit had expired. The pony was eliminated and with him the entire British team. The Canadians had now taken up the running and, when Jim Elder, their No 4, came in on The Immigrant, he had five fences in hand. He had four down, which was good enough for the team gold medals, though by any standards the penalty points, at $102\frac{3}{4}$ faults, were excessive, due to the exigencies of the course. France, for whom Janou Lefebvre and Rocket put up the best performance, were second on $110\frac{1}{2}$ faults. West Germany came third on $117\frac{1}{4}$ – a contributory factor was the showing of Alwin Schockemöhle on Donald Rex, who had the best score of the day, 4 faults plus $1\frac{3}{4}$ for time, and that of Hans Winkler on Enigk, for 12.

David Broome and Mister Softee had only three down, for a total score of 20 faults. Chapot and San Lucas, going last, could have given the United States the bronze medal if they had contented themselves with having three fences down, but two additional time penalties put them fourth to West Germany by $\frac{1}{4}$ fault.

It was a great triumph for the Canadians, a truly amateur team, after so many years of effort. Tom Gayford had $39\frac{1}{2}$ faults on Big Dee, Jim Day 36 on Canadian Club, and Jim Elder $27\frac{1}{4}$ on The Immigrant, thus breaking the stranglehold which the West Germans had exerted on the Olympic team gold medals since 1956.

8 Mexico to Munich 1969~1971

The feature event of the 1969 post-Olympic year was the Men's European Championship, held at Hickstead in July. This was the first year in which the FEI enforced the rule confining European championships to European riders – thus disqualifying Nelson Pessoa and the itinerant Americans and Australians – but was nevertheless a wise decision in that it gave enhanced status to the World Championship. This year, too, Hickstead was the trying-out ground for Ladbrokes, the London bookmakers, to introduce betting into show jumping – an unsuccessful experiment, owing to lack of support, and now discontinued.

Alwin Schockemöhle started a red-hot favourite on Donald Rex. After his triumph in Mexico City, Schockemöhle had won the German International Championship in Aachen, shared the Grand Prix on Wimpel with Winkler's Enigk, and won the Hamburg Jumping Derby on Enigk. He was quoted at 3 to 1 on the ante-post market, with Winkler second favourite at 7 to 2, d'Oriola third at 4 to 1 and Broome, the defending champion, fourth on the list at 5 to 1. Eight countries were represented, among them Italy with her previous winner, Raimondo d'Inzeo.

Broome and Mister Softee won the first leg, a speed competition, from Schockemöhle on Wimpel. Broome also finished third on his former Foxhunter champion, Top of the Morning, ahead of Winkler on Enigk. The second leg, judged over two rounds of a Nations' Cup-type course, had three joint winners on Schockemöhle on Donald Rex, Winkler on Enigk and d'Oriola on Pomone with Broome dropping to second place in the points race – one point behind Schockemöhle. The third leg was run over two courses: the first a tripartite course consisting of six speed, six puissance and six Cup-type fences; the second the same but with the puissance fences omitted leaving a dozen fences to be negotiated. Both Softee and Donald Rex went clear in the first innings, but Softee was some 3 secs faster, which actually won him the day. In the second innings Broome and Softee were clear again in a meteoric 65·8 secs; in trying to beat this time and discard the 3 secs lost in the first round, the German pair hit the last two parts of the treble. Softee was by now an old horse in terms of international competition, and this was to be his last season in the big time of the sport in which he made such a mark. After his victory, David Broome told

Alwin Schockemohle and Donald Rex, David
Broome's closest rivals in the 1969 European
Championship

me: 'I wonder if people realise how lucky they are to see a horse like that. He is the best I have ever ridden and I shall be lucky if I ever find another like him.'

The women's championship took place in Dublin. With only six starters, Anneli Drummond-Hay, the holder, was very well fancied to repeat her success, and Alison Westwood with The Maverick was second in the betting. Anneli won the first leg, on Xanthos, against the clock, with Iris Kellett on Morning Light second and The Maverick third. In the second leg, over thirteen Nations' Cup-type fences, Morning Light jumped two clear rounds to put Iris Kellett equal first with the defending champion. In the third leg, Morning Light's only faults were incurred in the water, but Xanthos had four fences down. So the European title went for the first time to an Irish rider. This was Iris Kellett's last year in the ring and the Dublin crowd gave her a great ovation.

France won her first Nations' Cup since 1964 at Nice with West Germany as runners-up. In Rome, the Germans won with 16½ faults against Britain's 20 and Anneli Drummond-Hay on Xanthos won the Trofeo Olgiata for the first Rome Jumping Derby. This trophy was the brain-child of an Hungarian cavalry officer, Count Laszlo Hunyady, who picked up an excellent command of the English language while a prisoner of war in Egypt. After the war he found himself working at Lord Derby's stud at Newmarket, on stable lad's pay, and learning the business from the bottom. When, years later, he married the daughter of Signor Tesio, the legendary Italian breeder of horses such as Ribot and Ribero, he was well qualified to run the Olgiata Stud, about 20 miles north of Rome, where the Derby was ridden over a cross-country type of course of natural and semi-natural fences. Count Hunyady died prematurely in 1971, and the Olgiata Derby died with him.

A British team, in which Trevor Banks's Hideaway, then ridden by Paddy McMahon, and George Hobbs's War Lord were representing their country for the first time, won the Nations' Cup in Barcelona with a zero score, France and West Germany following on. The Germans, making a determined

France's Janou Lefebvre on her thoroughbred, Rocket, winner of the Ladies World title in 1970 and 1974

Uncle Max, an ex-rodeo horse, whom even the equally-ebullient Ted Edgar sometimes found hard to handle

effort to record their first victory in the President's Cup won at Aachen, took the Prince of Wales Cup in London with a zero score, defeated Britain in a timed barrage for the Aga Khan Trophy in Dublin, and won again in Ostend. Germany received a slight setback in Rotterdam, coming only fourth, while Britain won from Poland, with the Netherlands third. In Geneva, already too far ahead to be in much danger of defeat for the world team title, the Germans set the seal on their success by winning the final European Nations' Cup of the season from Italy, who led at the halfway mark with a zero score but were slowly and systematically overhauled in the second half. Britain, who tied for third place with France, finished as runner-up for the President's Cup. Anneli Drummond-Hay, the Grand Prix winner on her previous visit to Geneva two years earlier, won four individual victories and two team relays, taking the City of Geneva trophy with the only clear round – one of Merely-a-Monarch's most notable performances.

Janou Lefebvre gave a foretaste of things to come when, on the thoroughbred Rocket, she won the Grand Prix and the championship in Nice, the John Player Grand Prix in

Harvey Smith coming down the Derby bank with
Mattie Brown to score the first of their two
consecutive victories in 1970

London, the Meisterspringen in Aachen, and the French Jumping Derby in La Baule.

Ted Edgar also hit the high spots, winning the King George V Cup in London on the grey American rodeo horse, Uncle Max, whom he had bought from Neal Shapiro. Uncle Max was an extremely difficult horse – even Bert de Nemethy, the brilliant coach to the American team, had failed to come to terms with him. He had confined him to the riding school at the team's training establishment in Gladstone, New Jersey, throughout the previous winter, hoping that by providing the initial schooling which the horse had never had, he could be made easier to control and his fantastic jump be used to the best advantage. De Nemethy had to admit failure when, as soon as Uncle Max was ridden out of the school, the horse reverted with a vengeance and bucked him off. Ted, an equally ebullient character, got on well with the horse, though when he was selected – against Ted's better judgement – for the British Nations' Cup team in Aachen Uncle Max gave him two crashing falls; yet, three weeks later, he won the King George V Cup. The Queen Elizabeth Cup went to Alison Westwood and The Maverick, with Anneli Drummond-Hay finishing second on Merely-a-Monarch for the fourth time.

Alan Oliver and Pitz Palu, a former notorious stopper who emerged as leading money-winner of the year, won the Ronson Victor Ludorum at the Horse of the Year Show for the second time running; Alan thus registered his ninety-eighth winning ride of the year.

On the North American circuit in the autumn, the United States won the Nations' Cups in Harrisburg and New York, but in Toronto Tommy Gayford, Jimmy Day and Moffat Dunlap, the Canadian team who had won the Olympic gold medals in Mexico, came out again to triumph over their neighbours. Jimmy Day won the Rothman's Canadian Championship (formerly the North American Championship) on his six-year-old Steelmaster, and the New York Grand Prix went to Dr Hugo Arrambide of the Argentine on Adagio.

In July 1970, the Nations' Cup in La Baule was held in conjunction with the Men's World Championship. The show attracted most of the best teams in the world, including Italy, the United States, West Germany and Britain, with a strong representation from the New World. France kept the flag waving and took Canada to a jump-off before ceding victory. The United States disputed third place with Britain followed by Brazil, Italy, Belgium, the Argentine, Mexico and Chile – a wonderful turn-out.

But it was the Men's World Championship which really drew the crowds. Britain was represented by David Broome with Douglas Bunn's Beethoven, and by Harvey Smith, who, riding Mattie Brown, won the first two qualifying legs. By this time Broome had dropped back to lie in seventh place on points over all, but he rallied in the third leg to win in beautiful style, thus qualifying for the final with Smith, Alwin Schockemöhle for West Germany on Donald Rex, and Graziano Mancinelli for Italy on Piero d'Inzeo's former Olympic horse, Fidux. A headstrong, excitable, hard-pulling horse, Fidux hotted up when Harvey Smith rode him, carting him into two wins of fences. All seemed lost for David Broome, who had still to ride him; but, in the three minutes allowed for coming to terms with a mount before jumping the course, Broome miraculously persuaded Fidux to settle, riding him like a show horse, with the reins as slack as a skipping rope, after passing a soothing hand down his neck. Fidux jumped the practice fence and then entered the ring without pulling an ounce, jumped a beautiful, calm clear round and won the day for Broome. Mancinelli and Broome had already jumped two clear rounds apiece, but Mancinelli had 4 faults at the water both on Mattie Brown and Beethoven, so that David had two fences in hand as he embarked on his final round with the best horse in the field, Donald Rex. Coming out of the treble, Donald Rex had the last part down, but Broome had already won the title, with Mancinelli second, Smith third and Schockemohle fourth.

Britain – with 20 faults to West Germany's 24 – had won the Nations' Cup in Rome, represented by Anneli Drummond-Hay with Merely-a-Monarch, Harvey Smith with the gargantuan Ten to Twelve, a half-Clydesdale, David Broome on Top of the Morning and George Hobbs on Battling Pedulas. Italy was third with 47, France fourth (58) and Spain last (92). The Grand Prix went to Piero d'Inzeo with Red Fox, a former winning show hunter in Dublin.

In Madrid, the Nations' Cup went to West Germany with 12 faults, France and Spain

Paul Weier of Switzerland reaches across Harvey Smith to congratulate Hartwig Steenken on winning the 1971 European title on Simona

were equal second on 16 and Britain fourth with 31. Ann Moore in her first big-time international show went well on the little Australian Olympic mare, April Love, with only 4 faults in each round over a really big course. Anneli Drummond-Hay won the Grand Prix with Merely-a-Monarch, who jumped three clear rounds and finally defeated Hans Winkler on Torphy by 2·7 secs.

The Americans arrived in Europe in time to compete at Lucerne, where they won the Nations' Cup with 8 faults to Britain's 12 and Germany's 16. The West German team was not at full strength, lacking Schockemöhle, Steenken and Winkler, while the Americans were fielding their best, among them Bill Steinkraus with Snowbound, now sound again, who was best individual with two clear rounds. The Grand Prix went to Captain Paul Weier of Switzerland, on Wildfeuer, with four clear rounds, and the runner-up was a newcomer to the British team, Raymond Howe, riding a veteran grey, Balmain.

The Russians went to Olsztyn to win the Nations' Cup with 23 faults to 28 for West Germany, who with Italy were the only non-communist nations in a field of seven teams, Britain having missed out the Iron Curtain circuit. The Prix des Vainqueurs went to

Hugo Simon for West Germany. Having dual nationality, Simon elected to ride for Austria in 1972 in order to compete in the Olympic Games.

In Aachen the home side won the Nations' Cup with only 4 faults to 12 by Britain, and the United States were third on 16, with Brazil, Italy, the Argentine and the Netherlands following on. Hermann Schridde took the Grand Prix on Heureka with four clear rounds, with Frank Chapot runner-up on White Lightning.

The 1970 Royal International in London was held indoors at the Empire Pool which kept the West Germans and the Americans away. The Prince of Wales Cup went to the home side: Mick Saywell on Hideaway – who had won the Grand Prix at La Baule with two clear rounds – Marion Mould on Stroller, Harvey Smith on Mattie Brown and David Broome on Beethoven, with 12 faults to 20 by Italy. Canada finished third with 28, followed by the Argentine, well behind on 63, Mexico even further in arrears with 92 and Sweden, who were eliminated.

Harvey Smith won the King George V Cup on Mattie Brown and Anneli Drummond-Hay finally captured the Queen Elizabeth Cup on Merely-a-Monarch. The Grand Prix for the John Player Trophy went to Marion Mould on Stroller, Raimondo d'Inzeo on the Irish horse Bellevue having the last word in the Daily Mail Cup, for which Stroller was runner-up.

Britain won the Aga Khan Trophy in Dublin, with 8 faults to Italy's 12, with West Germany third on 14½, France, Canada, Ireland and Sweden following on. Harvey Smith won the Grand Prix on Mattie Brown, his third clear round 1·7 secs faster than Raimondo d'Inzeo on Bellevue. Mattie Brown went on to stake his first claim to the British Jumping Derby at Hickstead after a jump-off with Alwin Schockemöhle on Donald Rex, who had a bad fall at the privet oxer.

The next port of call was Ostend, where Britain won the Nations' Cup with 18 faults to West Germany's 20; France was third on 31. In Rotterdam, Germany turned the tables, winning from Britain by 12 faults to 20 in a nine-team competition. In Lisbon, Switzerland swept the board, winning the Nations' Cup from Portugal (4 faults to 20), Spain and Italy. Finally, in North America, West Germany won in Harrisburg and New York,

with a zero score in Madison Square Garden against 4 for the USA. Despite Germany's successes, the President's Cup returned to Britain for the first time since 1967.

The Women's World Championship took place in late August in Copenhagen. Marion Mould was there with Stroller to defend her title, accompanied by Anneli Drummond-Hay and Merely-a-Monarch, with Ann Moore reserve on Psalm, a brown 16-hand thoroughbred. Janou Lefebvre of France on Rocket won the first round from Merely-a-Monarch and Stroller. After two clear rounds over a Nations' Cup-type course Stroller was tiring by the final round and Rocket prevailed. Stroller and Merely-a-Monarch were tying on points for second place, but Marion and Stroller were declared runners-up in view of their victory in the second leg.

David Broome, now without Douglas Bunn's Beethoven, who had back trouble, decided not to defend his European title in Aachen. Harvey Smith was an obvious choice of the selectors and to accompany him they opted for Mick Saywell and Hideaway – a fairly disastrous decision. The Aachen arena is a lovely showground, with permanent stabling and ample exercising and schooling areas, but when it rains the going becomes appalling. It rained for days before the championship, causing havoc in the preliminary speed competition. Hideaway, a half-Clydsdale, who had gone so well on equally rainsoaked but non-holding going in La Baule, was totally undone by the conditions underfoot. Pushed out of his leisurely natural rhythm in a competition where time was decisive, he had no fewer than eight fences down. Saywell retired his other ride, The Lodger, and the opening engagement fell to Paul Weier on Wulf for Switzerland, with Hartwig Steenken and Simona second for the host nation and Harvey Smith fourth on Evan Jones. Smith came further up the scale in the second leg, when Evan Jones and Mattie Brown shared first place with Raimondo d'Inzeo's gallant Bellevue, who had been withdrawn from the preliminary encounter.

In the final, Smith rode Evan Jones, and though the winner was d'Oriola on Moët et Chandon (formerly Iris Kellett's Morning Light), Hartwig Steenken had already accumulated sufficient points to win the title, with Harvey Smith as runner-up and Paul Weier in third place on Wulf. Steenken was a

universally popular and worthy winner of the European title. A farmer-breeder from Hanover, he is a most genuine, sporting and honest competitor, respected by his teammates and rivals alike.

The Women's European Championship took place in St Gall in Switzerland towards the end of August, but the reigning world champion, Janou Lefebvre of France, was conspicuous by her absence. Rocket was still recuperating from a back operation at the hands of a Swiss veterinary surgeon who specialises in the type of cure increasingly required by show jumping horses. Back troubles are one of the most prevalent unsoundnesses to beset international show jumpers today; they were unknown in the past. To satisfy the whims of the course-builders, horses must turn themselves inside out to negotiate fences which they are almost underneath for take-off. In view of the number of horses who spend weeks and months swimming round the Isle of Wight to get their backs into reasonable trim again, it could be one of the future tasks of the FEI to decide whether it is fair to ride a horse into the bottom of a fence and expect him to turn contortionist in order to reach the other side unscathed, or whether it is better to ask him to stand-off at a fence.

In St Gall, Ann Moore, who had just celebrated her twenty-first birthday, won the first leg on Psalm, with Alison Dawes finishing second and third on The Maverick and Meridian. The second leg was won by The Maverick, with Psalm and April Love – both ridden by Ann Moore – finishing second and third. In the third leg, Monika Bachman was lying third until she took the wrong course and was eliminated. Psalm made two mistakes, while The Maverick had a stop and a knock-down. Then Psalm gave Ann Moore a clear second round for victory, while The Maverick incurred a possibly controversial water fault. In third place was Monika Leitenberger of Austria.

In 1971 West Germany regained the President's Cup which she had won in 1969, and started her triumphant progress in Rome, which was the first CSIO (Concours Saut International Officiel) of the year – the French CSIO taking place at Fontainebleau instead of Nice. West Germany won the Nations' Cup with 16 faults to Britain's 20, with France third on 24 and Italy fourth on 28. Raimondo d'Inzeo took the Grand Prix on Fiorello and the Prix des Vainqueurs on Bellevue, while the Olgiata Derby, in its third and final year, was won by Graziano Mancinelli on Seamus Hayes's former horse, Doneraile, with David Broome runner-up on Beethoven.

Spain won the Nations' Cup in Barcelona with 8 faults, one fence better than West Germany and Britain, who tied for second place with 12; Portugal was a bad fourth with 89 faults. The Copa Generalissimo, equivalent of the Grand Prix, was won for Britain by Alison Dawes with The Maverick. Peter Robeson with Grebe finished third, below Karl-Heinz Giebmanns of Germany on The Saint.

In Fontainebleau, where an American team competed, West Germany reasserted itself to win with $5\frac{1}{4}$ faults from Italy with 13, Britain ($16\frac{1}{4}$) and the USA ($25\frac{3}{4}$), while the home side brought up the rear with 40. Ann Moore took the Prix de France on April Love, while the Grand Prix went to Germany's Alwin Schockemöhle on Donald Rex from Hartwig Steenken on Simona, with April Love third above Bill Steinkraus on Fleet Apple.

The winning German team of Winkler on Torphy, Steenken on Simona and Schockemohle on Donald Rex also included for the first time at a major international show Alwin's younger brother, Paul Schockemöhle, riding Askan, his own grey half-bred Hanoverian. Sold a few weeks later for the then record price of £56,000 to Josef Kun, an industrialist from the Ruhr, Askan was subsequently ridden by Gerd Wiltfang, a very determined and undoubtedly talented young rider with a somewhat dominating style. Since bought by Trevor Banks for Harvey Smith, Askan now has another forceful rider.

The next confrontation was at Aachen, where the United States eventually won the Nations' Cup after a jump-off with Britain. The Americans all went clear in the barrage, which Britain lost with 12 faults. The home side was third with 23½, followed by France (32), Italy (48), Russia (54¼), Spain, Switzerland, Poland, Belgium and the Netherlands.

The Grand Prix, with four clear rounds and finally 4 in the last barrage, was divided between Marcel Rozier of France on Sans Souci and Neal Shapiro of the United States on a most impressive bay thoroughbred called Sloopy, undoubtedly one of the best international novices of the year in this stage of his career. Once again, Ann Moore was Britain's only winner, taking two competitions on Psalm.

For the first time, Britain's Nations' Cup was contested outside London. The Hickstead July meeting was counted this year as part of the Royal International, though points were not awarded towards the President's Cup for the winners of the Prince of Wales Cup. This was unfortunate for Britain, as Harvey Smith on Mattie Brown, Alison Dawes on The Maverick, Graham Fletcher on Buttevant Boy and Stephen Hadley on No Reply won with a total of 4 faults to West Germany's 8. The Wills International Grand Prix went to Gerd Wiltfang on Askan, who – already a winner at this meeting – thus repaid his new owner a substantial part of his purchase price.

The second half of the show was held in London, where Askan went on to win the King George V Cup, while Marion Mould and Stroller beat Ann Moore and Psalm for the Queen Elizabeth Cup. The John Player Grand Prix went to Bill Steinkraus with Fleet Apple, the Daily Mail Cup to Hartwig Steenken on Der Lord, and the puissance was divided between Raimondo d'Inzeo on Bellevue and Anneli Drummond-Hay on Sporting Ford.

In Dublin, Germany won the Aga Khan Trophy from Britain in one of the closest finishes of all time, 33¼ and 33½ faults. Italy was third on 37½ and the United States fourth on 47, with Spain, France and Ireland following on. The German gladiators were held at bay in the Grand Prix by young Graham Fletcher on Buttevant Boy, while Ann Moore won the Guinness Gold Tankard as the leading rider of the week, having amassed the greatest number of points.

West Germany gave Ostend a miss, and the Nations' Cup was won by Ireland with 8 faults to Britain's 13¼. In Rotterdam, the Germans triumphed yet again with a zero score to Britain's 11 faults. Their next victory

Alison Dawes and The Maverick – outright
winners of the Generalissimo Cup in 1971

came in Budapest, a communist-state show which also attracted the Italians. In Lisbon the Nations' Cup was won by Britain from France, Italy and Switzerland, the winning score being 16 faults to 24 for France and Italy, equal second. Paul Weier, on Wulf, won the Grand Prix for Switzerland, and the Prix des Vainqueurs went to the Portuguese rider, Fernando Caldeira, on Gitana, from Piero d'Inzeo on Hans Winkler's former horse, Enigk, with Wulf third.

No European teams went to North America, the home side winning the Nations' Cup in Harrisburg from Canada and the Argentine with scores of $4\frac{1}{4}$, $8\frac{1}{4}$ and 32. The Grand Prix was won by Neal Shapiro with Sloopy. In New York, Canada prevailed in the team event, with 7 faults to 12 by the US team, and the Grand Prix went to Robert Ridland of the US on Almost Persuaded. In Toronto, Canada again prevailed, but the Rothmans Cham-

pionship fell to the attack of the veteran US horse, San Lucas, now ridden by Joe Fargis.

West Germany, who really deserved her President's Cup, had her final victory of the year in the Geneva Nations' Cup, with $8\frac{1}{4}$ faults to $12\frac{1}{4}$ by Britain, as usual the pace-maker. Spain, Switzerland and Italy followed on. Individually, the spoils were well shared between the nations, with Anneli Drummond-Hay's three victories the best of all, followed with two by David Broome on Manhattan and Gerd Wiltfang on Sieno. The Grand Prix was a triumph for Raimondo d'Inzeo with his future Olympic horse, the Italian-bred Fiorello.

Anneli Drummond-Hay, here on Big George, was a member of the 1972 British Nations' Cup team

9 Munich and After 1972~1974

The Munich Olympic Games, though sufficiently late in the year to enable the entire international season to progress more or less untramelled, nevertheless overshadowed every confrontation between horses and riders considered worthy of a place in the team. A short list of ten British horses and riders having been slected the previous autumn, Olympic trials were held at the Bath and West Show, the Royal Highland, the Great Yorkshire and at Hickstead, after which the team was announced. In 1972, for the first time, the Olympic Games followed the Nations' Cup formula of four horses and riders with the best three to count. First choice of the selectors was Mick Saywell with Hideaway, who had jumped the only clear round over a very stiff course at Harrogate. Ann Moore with Psalm was the probable second choice, followed by David Broome with Manhattan, and the fourth combination was Alison Dawes with The Maverick. But, after the Royal International, Mrs Dawes withdrew The Maverick, who was then unsound, and Harvey Smith was brought in with Summertime. Some critics questioned the wisdom of including Psalm, who had been known to stop in combinations; they considered him to be too small to cope with Olympic combinations, and harked back to Stroller's débâcle in Mexico.

In West Germany it was another story. There was bitter competition for a place in the team, and rescntmcnt built up ovcr the inclusion of Hans Gunter Winkler, by now considered a veteran. Some of the younger riders even said that, if he were selected, they would not ride with him. Eventually Winkler remained in, with Torphy, his team-mates being Hartwig Steenken with Simona, Fritz Ligges with Robin, and Gerd Wiltfang with the wonder-horse, Askan.

The United States team also had problems, Snowbound being no longer sound enough to be risked in the team event, Bill Steinkraus rode the young Main Spring. San Lucas was still active, but not as an Olympic prospect, and Frank Chapot partnered his wife's horse, White Lightning, while Kathy Kusner rode Fleet Apple. The fourth member of the team was Neal Shapiro riding the coveted Sloopy.

Italy had fewer problems than usual. Raimondo d'Inzeo had high hopes of his young Italian-bred Fiorello, and his brother Piero had a good young horse in Easter Light, though he lacked experience, with a second string in Red Fox, who was possessed of a gassy temperament and headstrong obstinacy on occasions. Mancinelli had Ambassador, a big grey Irish horse, and Vittorio Orlandi was going really well on another former Irish horse, Fulmer Feather Duster.

The Olympic season started in Nice, as usual, when a young British team – reinforced by Peter Robeson with Grebe and including Lionel Dunning with Aran Blaze, Simon Rogerson with Savannah and Stephen Hadley with Freeman – won the Nations' Cup from France, with 10 faults to $19\frac{1}{4}$. The Grand Prix de France went to Marcel Rozier on Sans Souci, who was beaten for the Grand Prix de la Ville de Nice by his compatriot, Marc Deuquet, riding Ulpienne, later a member of the Olympic team.

Except for the West Germans, who were keeping their powder dry, the big guns came out in Rome, where the home side won the Nations' Cup, fielding the d'Inzeo brothers on Fiorello and Red Fox, Orlandi with Valetta and Mancinelli with Ambassador. With a grand total of 12 faults, they won from Britain, who totalled 24 with a team consisting of Anneli Wucherpfennig (née Drummond-Hay) on Sceptre, Paddy McMahon on Penn-wood Forgemill, Alan Oliver on Sweep and Peter Robeson on Grebe. A 'second-eleven' team from West Germany finished third on 28 faults, with Brazil, Portugal, France and Belgium next in line.

Mancinelli won the Grand Prix on Ambassador, and Raimondo d'Inzeo took the Prix des Vainqueurs on Fiorello. Rome's Grand Prix follows a unique and rather questionable formula, with faults from the first round not carrying through to the second by the ten horses – or more in the event of equality – who go through. But Ambassador was indeed the moral victor, having jumped one of three clears in the first innings.

In Madrid, with five teams present, Britain and France jumped off for the Nations' Cup, which Britain won with 9 faults to an incredible $61\frac{3}{4}$, each team having an initial score of zero. Alison Dawes and The Maverick won the Generalissimo Cup for the third time, and thus outright, from Piero d'Inzeo on Easter Light and Peter Robeson on Grebe, but the Grand Prix, fought out by two Portuguese riders, went to the little-known Vasco Ramirez on Sire du Brossais, with the top British and

Two of the German contenders for the individual medal at Munich: Hugo Simon on Lavendel (seen here) and Hartwig Steenken with Simona (over page)

Italian riders finishing down the course – one of those turn-ups that keep show jumping full of suspense.

A return trip to Olsztyn in Poland by a three-man team of John Greenwood, Derek Ricketts and Stephen Pritchard gave Britain another Nations' Cup victory and more points towards the President's Cup, which they wrested from the West Germans by the slender margin of one point. Poland, on level pegging after two rounds, went under in the barrage. The Grand Prix went to the Polish rider Mrugala on Farsa, and John Greenwood was leading rider.

Aachen, intended as the final try-out for the British Olympic team, was to have been a real dress-rehearsal for Munich because both courses were being built by Hans-Heinrich (Mickey) Brinckmann. But in the event a British team did not go to Aachen at all. An outbreak of equine encephalitis in the southern United States barred the American horses from landing in England and the Ministry of Agriculture decreed that, if British horses went to Aachen and came in contact with the United States team, they would have to be quarantined on their return. The Italians also failed to send a full team, fielding only two individuals in the shape of Graziano Mancinelli and his wife, the former Nelly Pesotti, but eleven teams turned out, and though West Germany fielded her top riders with second-string horses she won the Nations'

Cup without any difficulty. In the Grand Prix, Winkler failed by only $\frac{1}{4}$ of a time fault to beat Nelson Pessoa on d'Oriola's former Olympic horse, Nagir.

For the Prince of Wales Cup in London the only teams to make the trip to jump indoors were a scratch Italian one and an even more ragged lot from Belgium. With Raimondo d'Inzeo the only visiting rider of any note, it was hardly surprising that the home side won with 4 faults from Italy's 28 and Belgium's 70·5. David Broome on Sportsman won his third King George V Cup and Ann Moore took the Queen Elizabeth Cup with Psalm. Harvey Smith and Summertime won the Grand Prix for the John Player Trophy, and David Broome the Daily Mail Cup with Manhattan.

For the first time since the Dublin show staged its first international competitions in 1926, there was no British team present, due to the troubles in Northern Ireland. West Germany, fielding a strong but non-Olympic team, retained the Aga Khan Trophy, beating Ireland by 8 faults to 32. The Grand Prix was won by Alwin Schockemöhle with The Robber from the Irish civilian rider, Eddie Macken, on Iris Kellett's Oatfield Hills. The British Jumping Derby went to Hendrik Snoek on Shirokko, the first-ever German winner of the Blue Riband of British show jumping.

The scene was finally set for Munich. Horses mustered in the stabling blocks at Riem and riders in the Olympic village two weeks before the start of the individual competition. The equestrian complex was superlative, with numerous dressage and schooling arenas, a magnificent covered school flanked by marble corridors, a smithy, a saddlery shop and even a circular wooden lungeing building. The stabling itself was unparalleled. The grooms, quartered above the big, roomy, air-conditioned loose boxes, could keep an eye on their charges through a window in the floor. There were push-button stable doors and an equine bathroom, with constant hot water, where horses could be hosed down without being exposed to draughts. Horses were stabled according to the nationality of their riders, which meant that the well-equipped saddle rooms were the scene of much chatting and coffee-drinking for the teams and their supporters.

The Olympic stadium was beautifully designed and seated a crowd of 30,000. The individual event provided a first-class warm-up for the Prix des Nations a week later. A field of fifty-five was reduced by one when Jan Kowalczyk's Chandzar died in his box overnight of a twisted gut, leaving the top Polish rider without a horse. Mickey Brinckmann had built an excellent course of fourteen fences for the first round, an unusual feature being the substitution of three doubles for any form of treble combination. The water, at No 11, was followed by a tricky turn into an oxer.

Three clear rounds eventually materialised – first from Jimmy Day of Canada on Steelmaster, then from Graziano Mancinelli with Ambassador, who went round with businesslike determination, and finally from Ann Moore and Psalm, whose performance was the most convincing of all, without a semblance of error.

The ten fences set for the second round were certainly formidable – big and solid and carrying immense spreads, though beautifully built. Measuring sticks were brought out to gauge the spreads and distances were paced by riders and camp followers alike. This round was fought out by the twenty highest-placed riders, which included all three British and all three West Germans. Saywell and Hideaway had 8 faults at the oxer following the water and at the last, while David Broome with Manhattan were also on 8, incurred at the seventh upright and the water, to which they took an angled approach. The West Germans had only one mistake apiece – Fritz Ligges and Robin at the water, Gerd Wiltfang and Askan at the last big oxer, and Hartwig Steenken and Simona at the fifth upright. It was sad that the defender of the gold medal, Bill Steinkraus of the United States, was not among the finalists; Snowbound was clear until the water, but erred again coming out of the double at 13 and then had the last fence down.

Alfonso Segovia's Tic Tac, after only one mistake in the first round, lost his consistency in the second for three mistakes, but Neal Shapiro with Sloopy was again round in 4, his only mistake coming at the penultimate oxer, 5ft 3in high with a spread of 6ft 10in. Jimmy Day and Steelmaster finished disputing fourth place, just out of the medals. Hugo Simon of Austria with Lavendel and, more surprisingly, Hartwig Steenken of West Germany with Simona were level with the Canadian pair at the finish. Then Mancinelli,

The respected sporting German, Hartwig
Steenken on Simona

on Ambassador, was faulted at the water and
hit a plank at No 8 on the run-in to the finish.
So Ann Moore and Psalm had only to get
round in 4 to take the gold, but the fates were
against them. At the second fence, upright
poles at 5ft 4in, Psalm took off almost per-
pendicularly, and Ann lost her irons. She had
to ride through the rustic double of oxers
without pedals and it was almost inevitable
that each element should fall. So, for the first
time since Helsinki, there was a jump-off for
all three medals against the clock.

Six fences were left in, and Neal Shapiro and
Sloopy were the first to go. They faulted at the
5ft upright going into the big treble, were
clear over the second upright and oxer which
came next, but hit the last fence for 8 faults in
46 secs. Mancinelli gave Ambassador no
quarter in this decisive final. Urging him on
into the treble after an about-turn on landing
over the wall, he seemed likely to pull the
horse's back teeth from their sockets, but
Ambassador did his best, was clear out of the
combination, flipped over the last fence and

was clear, a second faster than Sloopy to take up the lead.

Now it all hung on Psalm and perhaps Ann Moore tried too hard. He had no stride at all going into the second big upright and, as any sensible horse would do, he stopped. The next attempt gave him sufficient room to take off, and this gallant little horse was clear thereafter, to take the silver medal with 3 faults. But it was, though justice was done, a somewhat unsatisfactory ending to an Olympic contest.

There was a long wait before the team event, due to take place on the day of the closing ceremony – an interval marred by the horrifying terrorist outrage in the Olympic village. Finally, twenty-four hours later than planned, owing to a day of mourning for the Israeli victims, came the last contest of the Games. The weather, which had been sunny throughout, suddenly deteriorated. It was cold and wet when the first arrivals found their seats in Munich's Olympic stadium for the 8 am start of the Prix des Nations. The horses had left Riem before dawn and the riders had earlier walked the course – a big one of true Olympic quality. Once again

Vittorio Orlandi on Fulmer Feather Duster

Anne Moore and Psalm who came within three points of a gold medal at the 1972 Olympics

there were fourteen fences, including a double of uprights at 5ft 1in with a distance of 24ft 3in, and a treble. The main stumbling blocks were the double at No 4 and the combination at No 12, consisting of two big oxers 5ft high by 6ft 4in wide, with an upright at 5ft 1in coming out. Although the water was only 15ft 6in, it was to play a decisive role in the final stages.

Seventeen teams were in the line-up, and Vittorio Orlandi on Fulmer Feather Duster for Italy soon proved the course, going round in only 4, incurred at the treble. But the rest of the top teams came late in the draw. Fritz Ligges opened for Germany on Robin, and made only one mistake, at No 3, a parallel of planks standing at 5ft 1½in with a spread of 6ft 8in. For the USA Shapiro had the same fence down with Sloopy, and slipped while negotiating the U-turn into the following double, which led to a stop and 1¼ time faults. Then came Harvey Smith with Summertime, perhaps not a true Olympic horse, who performed depressingly for 16 faults; happily for Britain this proved to be the discard score, but it was not an encouraging start.

Despite the time lapse since the individual contest, many of the horses seemed jaded after their great effort – none more so than Mancinelli's Ambassador, who left the ring with five fences down. Piero d'Inzeo's Easter Light, who had been under the weather all the time he was in Munich, was going so badly that he was retired in each round. With these setbacks it was little short of miraculous that the Italians were able to rally their forces sufficiently to stay in the running.

The Germans made nothing of the combinations, but were caught out by some of the early fences. Gerd Wiltfang and Askan had No 3 down and the first part of the double, while Steenken and Simona only narrowly escaped without penalty in the double and treble, and finally paid the penalty at fence No 7, an oxer starting a line of three big fences on the far side of the course.

Kathy Kusner, back in the US team, had 20 faults with Fleet Apple in their first round. Frank Chapot, riding his wife's horse White Lightning in his second Olympic Games, was round in 8 to improve the position for the United States. Then Mick Saywell put up the best performance of the British team on Hideaway, who hit the same fences in each

Four times gold medallist Hans Winkler riding
Torphy in his last puissance at Wembley –
the reasons are self-evident!

round – the first part of the treble and the thirteenth fence: rustic parallels at 5ft 1in over a ditch with a spread of 6ft 8in.

Hans Winkler, the winner of four Olympic gold medals, justified his selection when, on the chestnut Torphy, he made his only mistakes at the first element of the two combinations. Thus West Germany finished the first round in front, with 16 faults, and would have been well clear of the field had it not been for Bill Steinkraus on Main Spring, who brought off the first clear round of the competition giving the US 16¼ faults.

Ann Moore and Psalm came unstuck at the treble; clear until then, he hit the first two elements and ran out at the third; though he jumped it faultlessly the second time, 11 faults accrued. David Broome raised Britain's flagging hopes with a 4-fault round on Manhattan, to bring the team's first-round total to 23, disputing third place with Spain. Although Sunday Beau, ridden by the Duque de Aveyro, was eliminated in each round, Segovia and Tic Tac with 4 and Martinez de Vallejo on Val de Loire with 7 put Spain ahead of Italy at this stage, when Raimondo d'Inzeo and Fiorello hit two fences.

The other teams to qualify for the second round were Switzerland (32·25), Canada (36) and the Argentine (41), for whom Jorge Llambi on O.K. Amigo had achieved the only other clear round in the first half. France, who had won the Olympic silver medals at Mexico and Tokyo, already had 80·25 faults; neither d'Oriola nor Janou Lefebvre had suitable horses. Moët et Chandon proved too erratic for an Olympic horse, and Rocket had not yet recovered from his back operation the previous winter.

West Germany and the United States widened the gap between themselves and their pursuers in the second round. Ligges nearly had a stop with Robin at the second fence of upright poles, but after this sticky beginning they were clear until the very last fence. Then Neal Shapiro and Sloopy jumped a classical clear round – the third and last of the competition – putting the US team ahead of the Germans. But Wiltfang and Askan redressed the balance, their only fault coming at the first part of the double.

Kathy Kusner reduced Fleet Apple's tally to 12. Simona, felling both parts of the double, was disappointing, but less so than White Lightning, who hit no fewer than seven

The hopes of America rested on Bill Steinkraus and Main Spring in the team event at Munich

fences. When Winkler's Torphy also hit the in and the out of the double, West Germany duplicated her first-round score of 16, for a total of 32 faults.

Now it was all up to Bill Steinkraus, forty-six years old and riding in his last Olympic contest. If he could achieve another clear round on Main Spring, he could lead the US team to its first-ever Olympic victory. The vast stadium was hushed as he embarked upon his crucial round. All went well until the water, where Main Spring did not rise a yard; a sickening splash, and it was all over. Though the rest of the fences were negotiated cleanly, Steinkraus – still the best individual for a total of 4 – captained the runners-up once again.

Now that the first and second teams had finished, with the destination of the gold and silver medals already decided, the sole remaining interest lay in the bronze medals of third place. The Spaniards were no longer in the reckoning, and Britain was being hard-pressed by Italy. Orlandi and Fulmer Feather Duster again had 4; Mancinelli had got Ambassador round with only two down, and Raimondo d'Inzeo, after Fiorello had hit No 3, rode him brilliantly round the rest of the course for no further penalties.

For Britain, Harvey Smith with Summertime were round in 4; Saywell and Hideaway were once again on 8. But Ann Moore had another disaster at the treble. Psalm hit the middle element and stopped at the third, then hit the first and stopped at the second. At his third attempt he went through clear, but 17 faults plus 3·5 for time spelt the discard score. It all rested upon David Broome and Manhattan, who had three fences in hand when they entered the ring if Britain was to win the bronze. Manhattan hit the second fence, the first part of the double, but then jumped faultlessly up to and including the treble. Then, with one fence in hand, this maddening horse elected to have the last two down, and Italy won the bronze medals.

On their way home many of the teams stopped off at Rotterdam, where West Germany beat Britain for the Nations' Cup in a desperately close-run thing, with 8 faults to 8¼. Rotterdam is surrounded by woods, which are close to the showground and sometimes

used for schooling – the sort of schooling which cannot be done in the open. Gerd Wiltfang was not the first rider to be reported for malpractice here; in 1967 a British rider was reported by, of all people, the Russians! On that occasion, the BSJA denied all knowledge of the affair. But when Wiltfang was reported, the West German federation took speedy action; he was sent home immediately, before the show was over, and rusticated for several months. He did not appear in any West German teams in 1973.

At the Horse of the Year Show the next month, Harvey Smith announced his intention of turning professional. He was the first to sign on in a four-nation professional circus which a theatrical *entrepreneur*, John Marshall, was trying to promote. The other members were Alwin Schockemohle, Raimondo d'Inzeo and Nelson Pessoa. They did not sign the final agreement, as a suitable sponsor could not be found, and after some months the project was dropped. It was made clear, however, by the Duke of Edinburgh, at the General Assembly of the FEI in Brussels in December, that if show jumping did not in the very near future put its house in order concerning 'shamateurism' it would be dropped as an Olympic sport. The BSJA had already set up a committee to discover how best the cause of the new professionals could be served; their recommendations were subsequently circulated to all the national federations, urging them to run a campaign on the same lines.

Early in 1973, the vexed question of amateur-professional status was tackled by the BSJA Secretary-General, Major Michael Dewey, who took a firm stand with those riders he considered to be professional. He was backed to the hilt by Harry Llewellyn and Sir Michael Ansell, whose chief concern was that Britain should come clean over her dubious amateurs, thus setting an example to the rest of the show jumping nations, and also that the new professionals should be enabled to make a good living.

Any rider competing in an international horse show had to produce an amateur permit or a professional licence. Those who were hesitating about taking the plunge which would debar them for ever from the Olympic Games were given temporary permits to enable them to ride at the indoor show in Berlin in the early spring. But most of the top-line international riders without any means of support other than riding and dealing in competition horses were given every encouragement to change their status.

Harvey Smith was the first to turn professional, followed in due course by David Broome and Ted Edgar, and eventually by several more. Ted Edgar, as a farmer, was a borderline case, but his association with the Everest Double Glazing Company, whose name was emblazoned on his horsebox, weighted the scales against him. By the time the 1973 season started, only Ann Moore and Graham Fletcher of the top internationals had had their amateur permits renewed.

It soon became apparent that none of the other nations had the smallest intention of following this lead. The first indication came when the committee of the Aachen show announced that no professionals would be allowed to ride in their Nations' Cup. Sir Mike Ansell wrote an admonitory letter and this decision was revoked, but that was as far as it went. West Germany is known to have several borderline professionals, including Hartwig Steenken, a farmer-breeder, but is reluctant to admit them, still less to take a firm line. Britain would thus be fielding a team of amateurs in the Olympic Games in Toronto in 1976, while Germany would endeavour to send her usual team, many of whom were to all intents and purposes every bit as professional as Broome and Smith.

Once again, at the FEI meeting in Brussels, the Duke of Edinburgh grasped the nettle and announced that, if other nations did not follow Britain's lead, he would have no alternative but to go to the Olympic Committee and tell them, with regret, that the FEI could not countenance the present situation and was powerless to alter it. This was tantamount to putting each national federation on its honour to put its house in order regarding show jumping, but it now seems doubtful that the position will be clarified in 1975.

The 1973 season was chiefly concerned with the European championships in which Britain regained the men's title, won at Hickstead by Paddy McMahon with Fred Harthill's Pennwood Forgemill; retained the women's title, with Ann Moore and Psalm winning again in Vienna; and in Belgium recaptured the Junior, thanks to the efforts of Debbie Johnsey – the Welsh girl originally selected for the Junior European team at the age of eleven – on her outstanding horse, Speculator.

Paddy McMahon, European Champion in 1973, and Pennwood Forge Mill, who began his jumping career by leaping out of a horsebox

Forgemill was bought for £140 as an unruly three-year-old, sold at the foal fair in Ballina, Co Mayo, and put in a open lorry with two others. At the border the driver declared three foals, but the customs officer shook his head and said: 'No, only two'. Forgemill had decided to jump out of the lorry and find his way home; he was caught six miles away on the roadside, with a wound on his shoulder – he still bears the scar.

Britain scraped home again in the President's Cup, after a tremendous struggle with the West Germans. The year started well when Ted Edgar led to victory in the Nice Nations' Cup a team consisting of Caroline Bradley, Lionel Dunning and John Greenwood. Riding Rhona's Boy, Greenwood won the puissance equally with Caroline Bradley on New Yorker, finishing second with Mr Punch for the Grand Prix to Johan Heins on Antrieb for Holland.

From Rome, Peter Robeson, Harvey Smith, Ann Moore and Lionel Dunning brought home the second Nations' Cup of the year, thanks very largely to a decisive clear round by Robeson with Grebe. On his Olympic horse, Easter Light, Piero d'Inzeo had two fences down to put Italy second, but this combination had a wonderful week, with four victories, including the Grand Prix and the Prix des Vainqueurs.

In Madrid Britain made a clean sweep, winning the Nations' Cup from the host nation and Portugal, with Paddy McMahon and Pennwood Forgemill the outstanding combination. They won on the first two days and went on to win the Grand Prix in an all-British finish, with Raymond Howe second on Fanta, Ann Backhouse third on Cardinal, and George Hobbs fourth on War Lord. Another successful partnership, and a new one this time, was that of Malcolm Pyrah with Mrs Gascoigne's Trevarrion, who won the Generalissimo trophy and also the Princess of Spain trophy, the championship of the show.

None of Britain's professionals wished to go to Aachen, which this year clashed with the Royal Show at Stoneleigh with its big sponsored prizes, but a young team of riders – including Graham Fletcher, Tony Newbery and Rowland Fernyhough – covered themselves with glory by finishing second to the

Alwin Schockemohle on Rex-the-Robber, a
highly successful combination at the Royal
International and Horse of the Year Show in 1973

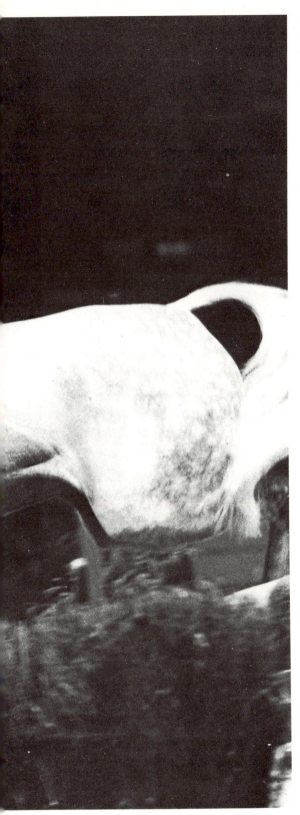

Germans in the Nations' Cup, by 8 faults to 24. Graham Fletcher on Buttevant Boy had only one fence down in his two rounds. Switzerland was third with 28, Italy fourth (48), with Belgium and Holland following on. Finally, Tony Newbery and Warwick, the ex-Australian horse he bought from John Fahey, tied with Alwin Schockemöhle and Rex-the-Robber as runners-up for the Grand Prix, behind Major Paul Weier of Switzerland on Fink.

At Hickstead, for the W. D. & H. O. Wills July International, incorporating the Men's European Championship, Britain's pair were Paddy McMahon with Pennwood Forgemill and Harvey Smith with Hideaway. The first leg of the title fight proved conclusively that the battle would lie between McMahon and Alwin Schockemöhle.

With thirty-one starters from eleven nations, including the Soviet Union, Schockemöhle staked his all on a fast clear round with his second-string, Weiler, in 91·6 secs, but Forgemill was more than a match for him, getting home in 90·7 secs, without penalty. Vittorio Orlandi filled third and fourth places for Italy with Fiorello (92·4 secs) and Fulmer Feather Duster (94·2). Schockemöhle's Rex-the-Robber hit the planks. With one point awarded for winners, two for runners-up and so on down the scale, only one point separated McMahon and Schockemöhle at the start of the second day.

In the first round, Harvey Smith and Hideaway pulled off the only clear, with Forgemill running out of steam coming out of the treble and joining eight others on 4 faults. In the second round, Hideaway went to pieces and had four fences down, leaving all the 4-faulters with a chance. Schockemöhle's Rex-the-Robber was the most dangerous, but his challenge evaporated when he pecked on landing over the water and turned a somersault, giving Alwin a fall.

Both the weather and the going deteriorated, and the 4-faulters all added 8 to their scores until Hubert Parot, the forty-year-old Frenchman, riding Tic, got round in 4. Forgemill finished among the six sharing second place, on 12 faults. All the equal seconds had 4·5 penalty points added to their overnight scores; thus Paddy McMahon had 5·5 to lead from Orlandi (7·5), Hugo Simon (8·5), Paul Weier (10·5), Parot (11), Harvey Smith (11·5) and Schockemöhle (13).

In the third leg, over a tripartite course of six speed, six puissance-type and six Cup-type fences – with the middle section omitted from the second round – Schockemöhle came storming back into an attacking position. The field was now reduced to fourteen, and first time round the only clears were jumped by Smith with Hideaway and Parot with Tic. Forgemill came unstuck at the first of the twin waters, but in the second round he was one of five with clear rounds to finish second, 13 secs in arrears of Rex-the-Robber. So, with only 2 points to add to his 5·5, McMahon became the undisputed champion of Europe, with Schockemohle second yet again on 14 and Parot third on 15.

Hugo Simon won the Grand Prix on Flipper for Austria before the scene shifted to the Empire Pool, Wembley, where Forgemill won the *Horse & Hound* Cup on the opening night of the Royal International and Harvey Smith on his German-bred, ex-Schockemöhle horse, Salvador, found a hole in the floorboards; fortunately, no one was hurt.

Forgemill, tailed by Hans Gunter Winkler with his Olympic horse, Torphy, went on to win the King George V Gold Cup with two clear rounds. The Queen Elizabeth Cup was shared, in identical times, by two former winners, Ann Moore with Psalm and Alison Dawes with The Maverick. Harvey Smith with Salvador won the Grand Prix from Schockemöhle on Rex-the-Robber, and David Broome finally entered the winner's enclosure via the Daily Mail Cup with Manhattan. Alwin Schockemöhle won both the saddle of honour (one horse) and the St George's Trophy (two horses). The Prince of Wales Cup – in which West Germany beat Britain with a zero score to 16 faults and 48 for the three Belgians – provided proof positive for the second year in succession that as long as Britain's Nations' Cup is held indoors in July the majority of the foreign teams in the top echelon will continue to bypass London.

In Dublin no applause could have been more generous than that accorded to the British team when they won the Aga Khan Trophy with a no-fault score to West Germany's $16\frac{1}{4}$, and with no discard score. McMahon and Forgemill – fresh from winning the Grand Prix in Belfast – Ann Moore with

The top American professional, Rodney Jenkins, and his top money-winner, Idle Dice

Psalm, David Broome with Manhattan, and Peter Robeson with Grebe were the heroes involved; their achievement may best be gauged by the fact that only Hans Winkler with Torphy managed even one clear round for West Germany in wet and slippery going. The Grand Prix went to Johan Heins of the Netherlands on Antrieb.

At the Horse of the Year Show, the Leading Show Jumper title went for the first time to David Broome, riding Sportsman; after which the international scene switched to North America. In Washington, the British team of Harvey Smith on Salvador, David Broome on Sportsman, Derek Ricketts on Tyrolean Holiday and Graham Fletcher on Buttevant Boy held the United States team to a jump-off before going under by a zero score, with West Germany third on $23\frac{3}{4}$. The Americans had three newcomers in Sam Kohne, Michael Matz and red-headed Rodney Jenkins, the top US professional, riding his thoroughbred, Idle Dice, probably the most coveted show jumper in the world at this time. The major individual championship went to Alwin Schockemöhle on Rex-the-Robber.

In New York, Britain achieved a great victory in the Nations' Cup, with 8 faults to 12 for West Germany and America, disputing second place, and Canada fourth on 24. The leading individuals were Rodney Jenkins with Idle Dice, and John Simpson of Canada riding Texas to a double clear round. The Canadians regard this seven-year-old chestnut quarter horse as a real find for their next Olympic team. Idle Dice won the Grand Prix from Graham Fletcher on Buttevant Boy and David Broome on Sportsman, and Harvey Smith took the international individual championship on Salvador and the leading foreign rider title.

At the Royal Winter Fair in Toronto, the United States won the Nations' Cup with $8\frac{1}{4}$ faults, conclusively defeating West Germany ($15\frac{1}{4}$), Canada ($16\frac{3}{4}$) and Britain (20). Rodney Jenkins and Idle Dice won two speed competitions and the Rothmans' Puissance, with the wall at 7ft 1in, from the Canadians, Moffat Dunlap on Scotch Valley, an Irish horse, and Jimmy Elder on Grande Nouvelle. The Grand Prix for the International Championship, sponsored by Rothmans, was won by Frank Chapot on Main Spring, with Rodney Jenkins, who emerged as leading international rider, second on Balbuco by 3·8 secs.

The two closest contenders for the World Championship of 1974: (left) Hartwig Steenken on Simona who eventually won from Eddie Macken on Pele (above)

At Geneva, the final European CSIO of the year, Malcolm Pyrah, Raymond Howe, John Greenwood and Paddy McMahon from Britain finished third for the Nations' Cup, won by West Germany with 16 faults to 20 for Switzerland. Hendrik Snoek won the Grand Prix on Rasputin from Hartwig Steenken on Simona. The final Grand Prix of the 1973 season, the Dunhill Victor Ludorum at Olympia in London, went to Graham Fletcher with Buttevant Boy.

In 1974 the President's Cup again went to Britain. The Men's World Championship at Hickstead was won by Hartwig Steenken on Simona for West Germany with Eddie Macken runner-up for Ireland on a remarkable former show hunter, Iris Kellett's seven-year-old

The last-ever winner of the Women's World title, Janour Tissot of France (left), and the runner up, Michele McEvoy of the USA (above)

chestnut, Pele. Frank Chapot on Main Spring for the USA and Hugo Simon on Lavendel for Austria finished equal third after Steenken and Macken had jumped off for first place.

The women's world title, the last ever to be contested – men and women now compete in an open world championship – was retained by Janou Tissot for France on Rocket. Michele McEvoy was runner-up for the United States on Mister Muskie, a quarter horse who died of pneumonia in Paris the following month, and Barbara Kerr on Magnor was third for Canada, just beating Britain's Caroline Bradley on True Lass.

British hopes took a blow when Ann Moore, twice winner of the European title, announced her retirement from the sport after Psalm went lame and had to rest for the remainder of the season. Marion Mould stepped into the breach, but her horses Dunlynne and John Gamble were not sufficiently experienced to present a challenge in La Baule. The Junior European title, won the previous year by Debbie Johnsey with Speculator, was taken by Ireland's James Kernan, sixteen-year-old son of the well-known dealer, Frank Kernan.

One of the features of the season was the brilliant success in Dublin of Raimondo d'Inzeo. Aged forty-eight, he rode his seventeen-year-old Bellevue to tie first in the puissance at 7ft 1in. Ultimately he won the Guinness Gold Tankard for the leading rider of the week.

David Broome was somewhat compensated for losing his world title when he won the Benson and Hedges Professional Championship, after a struggle with Rodney Jenkins at a new £18,000 show at Cardiff Castle, the first of an interesting series. Alwin Schockemöhle of West Germany, having been eliminated in the World Championship with Rex-the-Robber, had the consolation of winning, on the same horse, the amateur title.

The British Jumping Derby at Hickstead will go down in history as having been won for the third time by Harvey Smith, now on the German horse Salvador. And though the hero of the hour could not resist the temptation of making a jocular V-sign to Douglas Bunn when he came in to collect his trophy, this time it was all among friends, and the owner of Hickstead returned the gesture with interest, using both hands and grinning broadly. There is no doubt that Harvey has now matured in more respects than one. The old truculence

Top money-winners of 1974 – Harvey Smith and
Salvador

has gone – sublimated, perhaps, in the wrestling arena – and the new, relaxed Harvey Smith has doubled his following. Trevor Banks, his partner, attributes the new look to the fact that: 'He has pushed all his problems on to me. All he has to do is ride the horses!' Whatever the cause, the effect is excellent.

The season ended with two near-solid weeks at Wembley's Empire Pool – which must be the worst venue for international show jumping in the world. Now it was made even worse by the extensive building operations which were in progress throughout the fortnight, reducing the exercising space to the minimum, while cranes, dumper trucks and all the impedimenta of concrete progress plied their noisy, dusty trade in all directions. As one exhibitor said: 'It is like holding a horse show on a building site – I expect to be taken up in a crane at any moment!'

The ever-faithful Schockemöhle brothers and Jean-Michel Gaud of France ensured a minimal international flavour, both for the Horse of the Year and the Courvoisier Cognac shows, but the plums were plucked by the defending side. At the Horse of the Year, Harvey Smith won the Foxhunter Championship with Olympic Star; Caroline Bradley became the first woman ever to win a puissance, the Norwich Union on New Yorker, and David Broome won the Victor Ludorum on the American thoroughbred, Philco. The following week, the Courvoisier Cognac Supreme Horseman was Derek Ricketts, who won the £3,000 first prize in a qualified contest worth a record £9,000 in stakes, after riding all four qualified horses – Alwin Schockemöhle's Warwick, Harvey Smith's Harvest Gold, his own Tyrolean Holiday and Stephen Hadley's mare Flying Wild – in the final.

In September David Broome went to the States to jump in the San Diego Grand Prix in California with Sportsman and Manhattan – the latter re-named Jaegermeister, having been sponsored by the West German firm which makes an aperitif of the same name. He finished second for the big event to Rodney Jenkins of the home side on Number One Spy, but even so won £10,000 in prize money. He told me that he foresees more and more Europeans riding for big money in the United States, where the media has at last woken up to show jumping as a top sport. Hitherto, television and newspaper coverage has been minimal, even for competitions of Olympic and world championship calibre.

In Britain, the top money winner of 1974 was Harvey Smith with Salvador, who netted some £14,000 in stakes. The overall prize money increased by £93,000 to a record £414,000 thanks to numerous sponsors.

10 The Changing Face of Show Jumping

Show jumping has altered out of all recognition since those early days at the turn of the century. With the advent of professionalism – already well established in the United States – and with sponsorship and big money prizes a reality for well over a decade, it will change even more in the future. The cavalry officers who formed the earliest international teams have been replaced by farmers and horse dealers and businessmen whose horizon was at one time confined to the home front. Whereas in years gone by, few of the hard core of British show jumpers could be persuaded to travel abroad, now they are queueing up to catch the eyes of the selectors. Phil Oliver's famous saw: 'England's big enough for me' does not apply to the fathers of the younger riders, and this is just as well. For international successes in the numerous shows held all over the world help the sport enormously at home, and are indeed essential in its growth and prosperity. Sponsors would soon find other outlets for the money they spend on publicity if British riders were not good enough to beat their foreign rivals as often as they themselves taste defeat.

The sport has become infinitely more competitive, and therefore tougher, than it has ever been before. Horses do not last as long; they are harder to find and increasingly expensive to buy. A top horse could have been bought for £5,000 in the immediate post-war years. Now that sum is barely the price of a good novice. Nor does there seem to be any lack of demand, for with more and more people riding, and jumping at every level, competition horses and their production have become an industry on their own. At one time it seemed as though the sport could become over-exposed, with so many shows taking place throughout the year and so much television coverage, but it seems fairly certain that the big international events, where both riders and horses are household names, will always attract a good following, particularly in urban areas.

The most important requirements today are a strong and independent governing body, and stewards who can mete out justice without fear or favour. Every public attack levelled at show jumping has arisen from one premise: that some riders – a very small minority – employ dubious schooling methods which could, in some instances, be interpreted as cruelty.

Many people within the sport feel it is unfair that others should win competitions by methods which they themselves would hesitate to use. In the United States, an official 'rapper' is part of the scene; riders whose horses need a reminder to pick up their feet pay him a small fee to tap their horses with a bamboo cane, in public. In Europe such rapping is illegal. Yet some people are of the opinion that it is better for a horse to be given a gentle reminder in full view of all before he jumps than to be schooled at home, perhaps days beforehand, with no further reminder at the show.

Colonel Paul Rodzianko, who certainly had more experience of schooling jumpers than any man living, had an excellent schooling fence at the McKee barracks in Dublin. It consisted of light metal pipes, with a pulley arrangement at the side. When a horse grew careless, the pulley was operated as he took off, and when he hit the pipe it made a noise which he disliked, without hurting him in the least. No one, even the most ardent protector of horses, could consider this method to be cruel – but it would not be allowed at any horse show.

Rodzianko had a real love for horses, but insisted that they should be properly trained, properly ridden, and obedient and under control at all times. 'More cruelty is inflicted upon horses by ignorant riders who know nothing of training, and of the basic principles of riding,' he told me, 'than by the most ambitious educated horseman.'

The lack of adequately qualified trainers, since cavalry regiments were mechanised, is already making itself felt. The situation will worsen in the next ten years, when the few remaining cavalrymen pass on. Who will then be able to take their place in passing on the knowledge accumulated over the years on the specialist subject of show jumping? Perhaps the most likely people will be the new professionals when they have retired from the ring.

OLYMPIC GAMES

Paris 1900

Prize Jumping (1) Haegeman (Belgium)
(2) Van der Poele (Belgium)
(3) De Champsavin (France)

High Jump (1) Gardere (France) 6ft 13/16in
(2) G. Trissino (Italy)

Long Jump (1) Van Langendonck (Belgium) 20ft 1/16in
(2) G. Trissino (Italy)

Stockholm 1912

Team (1) Sweden: Count Casimir Lewenhaupt on Medusa; Count Hans von Rosen on Lord Iron; Lt Frederick Rosencrantz on Drabant; Lt Gustaf Kilman on Gatan
(2) France: Lt d'Astaford on Amazone; Capt J. Cariou on Mignon; Comdt F. Meyer on Allons V; Lt Seigneur on Cocotte
(3) Germany: Capt Sigismund Freyer on Ultimus; Graf von Hohenau on Pretty Girl; Lt Deloch on Hubertus; Prinz Karl von Preussen on Gibson Boy

Individual (1) Capt J. Cariou (France) on Mignon (2) Lt von Krocher (Germany) on Dohna (3) Baron E. Blommaert de Soye (Belgium) on Clonmore

Antwerp 1920

Team (1) Sweden: Count Hans von Rosen; C. Konig; Daniel Norling
(2) Belgium: Capt Count de Oultremont; Lt Coumans; Baron de Gaiffier
(3) Italy: Magg Ettore Caffaratti; Giulio Cacciandra; Magg Allessandro Alvisi

Individual (1) Lt Tomasso Lequio on Trebecco (Italy) (2) Magg Allessandro Valerio on Cento (Italy) (3) Capt Gustaf Lewenhaupt on Mon Coeur (Sweden)

Paris 1924

Team (1) Sweden: Ake Thelning on Loke; Axel Stahle on Cecil; Age Lundstrom
(2) Switzerland: Lt Alphons Gemuseus on Lucette; Werner Stuber; Hans Buhler
(3) Portugal: Borges d'Almeida on Reginald; Martins de Souza; Mouzinho d'Alberquerque

Individual (1) Lt Alphons Gemuseus on Lucette (Switzerland) (2) Lt Tomasso Lequio on Trebecco (Italy) (3) Lt Adam Krolikiewicz on Picador (Poland)

Amsterdam 1928

Team (1) Spain: Marquis de los Trujillos on Zalermo; J. Navarro Morenes on Zapatazo; J. Garcia Fernandez on Revistade
(2) Poland: C. Gzowki on Mylord; K. Szoszland on Alli; M. Antoniewicz on Readglet
(3) Sweden: K. Hansen on Gerold; C. Bjornstjerna on Kornett; Ernst Hallberg on Loke

Individual (1) Capt F. Ventura on Eliot (Czechoslovakia) (2) Capt M. L. M. Bertran de Balanda on Papillon (France) (3) Major Chasimir Kuhn on Pepita (Switzerland)

Los Angeles 1932

Team Not awarded as no team completed the course

Individual (1) Lt Baron Takeichi Nishi on Uranus (Japan) (2) Major Harry Chamberlin on Show Girl (USA) (3) Lt Clarence von Rosen on Empire (Sweden)

Berlin 1936

Team (1) Germany (44 faults): Lt Kurt Hasse on Tora; Capt Martin von Barnekow on Nordland; Capt Heinz Brandt on Alchimist
(2) Holland (51½ faults): Lt Johan Greter on Ernica; Lt Jan de Bruine on Trixie; Lt Henri van Schaik on Santa Bell
(3) Portugal (56 faults): Lt Jose Beltrano on Biscuit; Capt Marquez de Funchal on Merle Blanc; Lt Manae e Silva on Fossette

Individual (1) Lt Kurt Hasse on Tora (Germany) (2) Lt Henri Rang on Delphis (Rumania) (3) Capt Jozsef Platthy on Selloe (Hungary)

London 1948

Team (1) Mexico (34¼ faults): Col Humberto Mariles Cortez on Arete; Lt Ruben Uriza on Hatuey; Alberto Valdes on Chihuahua
(2) Spain (56½ faults): Cmdt Jaime Garcia Cruz on Bizarro;

Col. Morenes Navarro on Quorum; Cmdt G. y Ponce de Leon on Foregido

(3) Great Britain (67 faults): Lt-Col Harry Llewellyn on Foxhunter; Lt-Col Henry Nicoll on Kilgeddin; Major Arthur Carr on Monty

Individual (1) Col H. Mariles Cortez on Arete (Mexico) 6¼f (2) Ruben Uriza on Hatuey (Mexico) 8f–zero in jump off (3) Chev J. F. M. d'Orgeix on Sucre de Pomme (France) 8f–4f

Helsinki 1952
Team (1) Great Britain (40¾ faults): Col H. M. Llewellyn on Foxhunter; W. H. White on Nizefela; Col D. N. Stewart on Aherlow

(2) Chile (45¾ faults): Oscar Cristi on Bambi; C. Mendoza on Pillan; Ricardo Echeverria on Lindo Peal

(3) USA (52¼ faults): W. C. Steinkraus on Hollandia; John Russell on Democrat; Arthur McCashin on Miss Budweiser

Individual (1) Pierre Jonquères d'Oriola on Ali Baba (France) 8f–zero in 40secs in barrage (2) Oscar Christi on Bambi (Chile) 8f–4f in 44secs (3) Fritz Thiedemann on Meteor (West Germany) 8f–8f in 38·5secs

Stockholm 1956
Team (1) West Germany (40 faults): Hans Gunter Winkler on Halla; Fritz Thiedemann on Meteor; Alf. Lutke-Westhues on Ala

(2) Italy (66 faults): Capt Raimondo d'Inzeo on Merano; Capt Piero d'Inzeo on Uruguay; Capt Salvatore Oppes on Pagoro

(3) Great Britain (69 faults): Wilf White on Nizefela; Pat Smythe on Flanagan; Peter Robeson on Scorchin'

Individual (1) Hans Gunter Winkler on Halla (West Germany) 4f (2) Capt R. d'Inzeo on Merano (Italy) 8f (3) Capt P. d'Inzeo on Uruguay (Italy) 11f

Rome 1960
Team (1) West Germany (46½ faults): Alwin Schockemohle on Ferdl; Hans Winkler on

Major Raimondo d'Inzeo

Halla; Fritz Thiedemann on
Meteor
(2) USA (66 faults): W. C. Stein-
kraus on Ksar d'Esprit;
Frank Chapot on Trail
Guide; George Morris on
Sinjon
(3) Italy (80½ faults): Capt R.
d'Inzeo on Posillipo; Capt
P. d'Inzeo on The Rock;
Capt A. Oppes on The
Scholar

Individual   (1) Capt R. d'Inzeo on Posillipo
(Italy) 12f (2) Capt P.
d'Inzeo on The Rock (Italy)
16f (3) D. Broome on Sun-
salve (GB) 23f

Tokyo 1964
Team   (1) West Germany (68½ faults):
Hermann Schridde
on Dozent; Kurt Jarasinski on
Torro; Hans Gunter Winkler
on Fidelitas
(2) France (77¾ faults): P. J.
d'Oriola on Lutteur B; Capt
Guy Lefrant on M. de Littry;
Janou Lefebvre on Rocket
(3) Italy (88½ faults): Capt P.
d'Inzeo on Sunbeam; Capt
R. d'Inzeo on Posillipo;
Graziano Mancinelli on
Rockette

Individual   (1) P. J. d'Oriola on Lutteur B
(France) 9f (2) H. Schridde
on Dozent (West Germany)
13¾f (3) P. Robeson on Firecrest (GB) 16f

Mexico City 1968
Team   (1) Canada (102¾ faults): Jimmy
Day on Canadian Club; Jim
Elder on The Immigrant;
Tommy Gayford on Big Dee
(2) France (110½ faults): P. J.
d'Oriola on Nagir; Janou
Lefebvre on Rocket; Marcel
Rozier on Quo Vadis
(3) West Germany (117¼ faults):
H. Schridde on Dozent;
H. G. Winkler on Enigk; A.
Schockemohle on Donald
Rex

Individual   (1) W. C. Steinkraus on Snowbound (USA) 4f (2) Marion
Coakes on Stroller (GB) 8f
(3) D. Broome on Mister
Softee (GB) 12f

Munich 1972
Team   (1) West Germany (32 faults): F.
Ligges on Robin; G. Wilt-
fang on Askan; H. Steenken
on Simona; H. G. Winkler
on Torphy
(2) USA (32·25 faults): W. C.

Steinkraus on Main Spring;
N. Shapiro on Sloopy;
Kathy Kusner on Fleet
Apple; F. Chapot on White
Lightning
(3) Italy (48 faults): Dr V.
Orlandi on Fulmer Feather
Duster; Capt R. d'Inzeo on
Fiorello II; G. Mancinelli
on Ambassador; Major P.
d'Inzeo on Easter Light
(Italy) 8f–zero (2) Ann
Moore on Psalm (GB) 8f–3f
(3) Neal Shapiro on Sloopy

Individual   (1) G. Mancinelli on Ambassador
(USA) 8f–8f

MEN'S WORLD CHAMPIONSHIP

Paris 1953   (1) F. Goyoaga on Quorum
(Spain)
(2) F. Thiedemann on Diamant
(W. Germany)
(3) P. J. d'Oriola on Ali Baba
(France)
(4) Capt P. d'Inzeo on Uruguay
(Italy)

Madrid 1954   (1) H. G. Winkler on Halla (W.
Germany)
(2) P. d'Oriola on Arlequin D
(France)
(3) F. Goyoaga (Spain) to final
as holder
(4) S. Oppes on Pagoro (Italy)

Aachen 1955   (1) H. G. Winkler on Halla (W.
Germany)
(2) Capt R. d'Inzeo on Nadir
(Italy)
(3) Major R. Dallas on Bones
(GB)
(4) P. J. d'Oriola (France) retired

Aachen 1956   (1) Capt R. d'Inzeo on Merano
(Italy)
(2) F. Goyoaga on Fahnenkönig
(Spain)
(3) F. Thiedemann on Meteor
(W. Germany)
(4) Col C. Delia on Discutido
(the Argentine)

Venice 1960   (1) Capt R. d'Inzeo on Gowran
Girl (Italy)
(2) Col C. Delia on Huipil (the
Argentine)
(3) D. Broome on Sunsalve (GB)

(4) W. C. Steinkraus on Ksar
d'Esprit (USA)

Buenos Aires 1966   (1) P. J. d'Oriola on Pomone
(France)
(2) A. de Bohorques on Quizas
(Spain)
(3) Capt R. d'Inzeo on Bowjack
(Italy)

(4) N. Pessoa on Huipil (Brazil)

La Baule 1970
(1) D. Broome on Beethoven (GB)
(2) G. Mancinelli on Fidux (Italy)
(3) H. Smith on Mattie Brown (GB)
(4) A. Schockemohle on Donald Rex (W. Germany)

Hickstead 1974
(1) H. Steenken on Simona (W. Germany)
(2) E. Macken on Pele (Ireland)
(3) F. D. Chapot on Main Spring (USA) and H. Simon on Lavendel (Austria)

MEN'S EUROPEAN CHAMPIONSHIP

Rotterdam 1957
(1) H. G. Winkler on Sonnenglanz (W. Germany)
(2) Capt B. de Fombelle on Bucephale (France)
(3) Capt S. Oppes on Pagoro (Italy)

Aachen 1958
(1) F. Thiedemann on Meteor (W. Germany)
(2) Capt R. d'Inzeo on The Rock (Italy)
(3) H. G. Winkler on Halla (W. Germany)

Paris 1959
(1) Capt P. d'Inzeo on Uruguay (Italy)
(2) P. J. d'Oriola on Virtuoso (France)
(3) F. Thiedemann on Godewind (W. Germany)

1960
Not held

Aachen 1961
(1) D. Broome on Sunsalve (GB)
(2) Capt P. d'Inzeo on Pioneer (Italy)
(3) H. G. Winkler on Romanus (W. Germany)

London 1962
(1) C. D. Barker on Mister Softee (GB)
(2) H. G. Winkler on Romanus (W. Germany) and Capt P. d'Inzeo on The Rock (Italy)

Rome 1963
(1) G. Mancinelli on Rockette (Italy)
(2) A. Schockemohle on Freiherr (W. Germany)
(3) H. Smith on O'Malley (GB)

1964
Not held

Graziano Mancinelli of Italy

Brazil's Nelson Pessoa

Aachen 1965	(1) H. Schridde on Dozent (W. Germany)		(2) A. Schockemohle on Donald Rex (W. Germany)
	(2) N. Pessoa on Gran Geste (Brazil)		(3) H. G. Winkler on Enigk (W. Germany)
	(3) A. Schockemohle on Exakt (W. Germany)	**1970**	Not held
Lucerne 1966	(1) N. Pessoa on Gran Geste (Brazil)	**Aachen 1971**	(1) H. Steenken on Simona (W. Germany)
	(2) F. Chapot on San Lucas (USA)		(2) H. Smith on Evan Jones (GB)
	(3) H. Arrambide on Chimbote (the Argentine)		(3) Major Paul Weier on Wulf (Switzerland)
		1972	Not held
Rotterdam 1967	(1) D. Broome on Mister Softee (GB)	**Hickstead 1973**	(1) Paddy McMahon on Pennwood Forgemill (GB)
	(2) H. Smith on Harvester (GB)		(2) A. Schockemohle on Rex-the-Robber (W. Germany)
	(3) A. Schockemohle on Donald Rex (W. Germany)		(3) H. Parot on Tic (France)
1968	Not held	**1974**	Not held
Hickstead 1969	(1) D. Broome on Mister Softee (GB)		

WOMEN'S WORLD CHAMPIONSHIP

Hickstead 1965
(1) Miss M. Coakes on Stroller (GB)
(2) Miss K. Kusner on Untouchable (USA)
(3) Miss A. Westwood on The Maverick (GB)

Copenhagen 1970
(1) Miss J. Lefebvre on Rocket (France)
(2) Mrs D. Mould on Stroller (GB)
(3) Miss A. Drummond-Hay on Merely-a-Monarch (GB)

La Baule 1974
(1) Mme J. Tissot on Rocket (France)
(2) Miss M. McEvoy on Mister Muskie (USA)
(3) Mrs B. Simpson Kerr on Magnor (Canada)

WOMEN'S EUROPEAN CHAMPIONSHIP

Spa 1957
(1) Miss P. Smythe on Flanagan (GB)
(2) Miss G. Serventi on Doly (Italy)
(3) Mme M. d'Orgeix on Ocean (France)

Palermo 1958
(1) Miss G. Serventi on Doly (Italy)
(2) Miss A. Clement on Nico (W. Germany)
(3) Miss I. Jansen on Adelboom (Holland)

Rotterdam 1959
(1) Miss A. Townsend on Bandit (GB)
(2) Miss P. Smythe on Flanagan (GB)
(3) Miss A. Clement on Nico (W. Germany) and Miss G. Serventi on Doly (Italy)

Copenhagen 1960
(1) Miss S. Cohen on Clare Castle (GB)
(2) Mrs W. Wofford on Hollandia (GB)
(3) Miss A. Clement on Nico (W. Germany)

Deauville 1961
(1) Miss P. Smythe on Flanagan (GB)
(2) Miss I. Jansen on Icare (Holland)
(3) Miss M. Cancre on Ocean (France)

Madrid 1962
(1) Miss P. Smythe on Flanagan (GB)
(2) Mrs H. Kohler on Cremona (W. Germany)
(3) Mrs P. Goyoaga on Kif Kif (Spain)

Hickstead 1963
(1) Miss P. Smythe on Flanagan (GB)

(2) Mrs A. Givaudan on Huipil (Brazil)
(3) Miss A. Drummond-Hay on Merely-a-Monarch (GB)

1964 Not held

Gijon 1966
(1) Miss J. Lefebvre on Kenavo D (France)
(2) Miss M. Backmann on Sandro (Switzerland)
(3) Miss L. Novo on Oxo Bob (Italy)

Fontainebleau 1967
(1) Miss K. Kusner on Untouchable (USA)
(2) Miss L. Novo on Predestine (Italy)
(3) Miss M. Bachmann on Erbach (Switzerland)

Rome 1968
(1) Miss A. Drummond-Hay on Merely-a-Monarch (GB)
(2) Miss G. Serventi on Gay Monarch (Italy)
(3) Miss M. Coakes on Stroller (GB) and Miss J. Lefebvre on Rocket (France)

Dublin 1969
(1) Miss I. Kellett on Morning Light (Ireland)
(2) Miss A. Drummond-Hay on Xanthos (GB)
(3) Miss A. Westwood on The Maverick (GB)

St Gall 1971
(1) Miss A. Moore on Psalm (GB)
(2) Mrs M. Dawes on The Maverick (GB)
(3) Miss M. Leitenberger on Limbarra de Porto Conte (Austria)

PRESIDENT'S CUP
World team championship, won on points gained in each country's six best Nations' Cup results

1965
(1) GB
(2) W. Germany
(3) Italy

1966
(1) USA
(2) Spain
(3) France

1967
(1) GB
(2) W. Germany
(3) Italy

1968
(1) USA
(2) GB
(3) Italy and W. Germany

1969
(1) W. Germany
(2) GB
(3) Italy

1970
(1) GB
(2) W. Germany
(3) Italy

1971	(1)	W. Germany
	(2)	GB
	(3)	Italy
1972	(1)	GB
	(2)	W. Germany
1973	(1)	GB
	(2)	W. Germany
	(3)	Italy
1974	(1)	GB
	(2)	W. Germany
	(3)	Italy

BRITISH JUMPING DERBY
(sponsored by W. D. & H. O. Wills)

1961	Seamus Hayes on Goodbye (Ireland)
1962	Miss P. Smythe on Flanagan (GB)
1963	N. Pessoa on Gran Geste (Brazil)
1964	S. Hayes on Goodbye (Ireland)
1965	N. Pessoa on Gran Geste (Brazil)
1966	D. Broome on Mister Softee (GB)
1967	Miss M. Coakes on Stroller (GB)
1968	Miss A. Westwood on The Maverick (GB)
1969	Miss A. Drummond-Hay on Xanthos (GB)
1970	H. Smith on Mattie Brown (GB)
1971	H. Smith on Mattie Brown (GB)
1972	H. Snoek on Shirokko (W. Germany)
1973	Mrs M. Dawes on Mr Banbury (formerly The Maverick)
1974	H. Smith on Salvador (GB)

KING GEORGE V GOLD CUP

1911	Capt D. d'Exe on Piccolo (Russia)
1912	Lt Delvoie on Murat (Belgium)
1913	Lt Baron de Meslon on Amazone (France)
1914	Lt Baron de Meslon on Amazone (France)
1920	Capt de Laissardière on Dignité (France)
1921	Lt-Col Geoffrey Brooke on Combined Training (GB)
1922	Major Count Antonelli on Bluff (Italy)
1923	Capt de Laissardière on Grey Fox (France)
1924	Capt Count Borsarelli on Don Chisciotte (Italy)
1925	Lt-Col Malise Graham on Broncho (GB)
1926	Lt F. H. Bontecou on Ballymacshane (USA)
1927	Lt X. Bizard on Quinine (France)
1928	Lt A. G. Martyr on Forty-Six (France)
1929	Lt Gibault on Mandarin (France)
1930	Lt J. A. Talbot-Ponsonby on Chelsea (GB)
1931	Capt J. Misonne on The Parson (Belgium)
1932	Lt J. A. Talbot-Ponsonby on Chelsea (GB)
1933	No Show
1934	Lt J. A. Talbot-Ponsonby on Best Girl (GB)
1935	Capt J. J. Lewis on Tramore Bay (Ireland)
1936	Comdt J. G. O'Dwyer on Limerick Lace (Ireland)
1937	Capt Xavier Bizard on Honduras (France)
1938	Major J. C. Friedberger on Derek (GB)
1939	Lt A. Bettoni on Adigrat (Italy)
1947	P. J. d'Oriola on Marquis III (France)
1948	Lt-Col H. M. Llewellyn on Foxhunter (GB)
1949	Brian Butler on Tankard (GB)
1950	Lt-Col H. M. Llewellyn on Foxhunter (GB)
1951	Capt Kevin Barry on Ballyneety (Ireland)

1952	Don Carlos Figueroa on Gracieux (Spain)
1953	Lt-Col H. M. Llewellyn on Foxhunter (GB)
1954	F. Thiedemann on Meteor (W. Germany)
1955	Lt-Col Cartasegna on Brando (Italy)
1956	W. C. Steinkraus on First Boy (USA)
1957	Capt P. d'Inzeo on Uruguay (Italy)
1958	H. Wiley on Master William (USA)
1959	H. Wiley on Nautical (USA)
1960	D. Broome on Sunsalve (GB)
1961	Capt P. d'Inzeo on The Rock (Italy)
1962	Capt P. d'Inzeo on The Rock (Italy)
1963	T. Wade on Dundrum (Ireland)
1964	W. C. Steinkraus on Sinjon (USA)
1965	H. G. Winkler on Fortun (W. Germany)
1966	D. Broome on Mister Softee (GB)
1967	P. Robeson on Firecrest (GB)
1968	H. G. Winkler on Enigk (W. Germany)
1969	T. H. Edgar on Uncle Max (GB)
1970	H. Smith on Mattie Brown (GB)
1971	G. Wiltfang on Askan (W. Germany)
1972	D. Broome on Sportsman (GB)
1973	P. McMahon on Pennwood Forgemill (GB)
1974	F. D. Chapot on Main Spring (USA)

QUEEN ELIZABETH II CUP

1949	Miss Iris Kellett on Rusty (Ireland)
1950	Miss Jill Palethorpe on Silver Cloud (GB)
1951	Miss Iris Kellett on Rusty (Ireland)
1952	Mrs George Rich on Quicksilver III (GB)
1953	Miss Marie Delfosse on Fanny Rosa (GB)
1954	Miss José Bonnaud on Charleston (France)
1955	Miss Dawn Palethorpe on Earlsrath Rambler (GB)
1956	Miss Dawn Palethorpe on Earlsrath Rambler (GB)
1957	Miss Elizabeth Anderson on Sunsalve (GB)
1958	Miss Pat Smythe on Mr Pollard (GB)
1959	Miss Anna Clement on Nico (W. Germany)
1960	Miss Sue Cohen on Clare Castle (GB)
1961	Lady Sarah Fitzalan-Howard on Oorskiet (GB)
1962	Mrs Brian Crago on Spring Fever (GB)
1963	Miss Julie Nash on Trigger Hill (GB)
1964	Miss Gillian Makin on Jubilant (GB)
1965	Miss Marion Coakes on Stroller (GB)
1966	Miss Althea Roger Smith on Havana Royal (GB)
1967	Miss Betty Jennaway on Grey Leg (GB)
1968	Mrs Frank Chapot on White Lightning (USA)
1969	Mrs Michael Dawes on The Maverick (GB)
1970	Miss Anneli Drummond-Hay on Merely-a-Monarch (GB)
1971	Mrs David Mould on Stroller (GB)
1972	Miss Ann Moore on Psalm (GB)
1973	Miss Ann Moore on Psalm and Mrs Michael Dawes on Mr Banbury (formerly The Maverick) (both GB)
1974	Mrs Stephen Davenport on All Trumps (GB)

Harvey Smith and Salvador, winners of the 1974 British Jumping Derby

Index